To Beata with love Basia xx

SEXTY SOMETHING

The story of a woman who ended up on TOP in business and in life!

DON'T GET YOUR KNICKERS IN A TWIST

BY BASIA

Written with Kevin O'Donnell

ISBN - 1450529690
EAN - 9781450529693

Printed in the United States of America

My Legacy Press (www.mylegacypress.com)

PREFACE

My life began in troubled times, in a city at the epicenter of an ancient crusade. I was a stateless child, living in Jerusalem, but connected to a Polish lineage that stretched back a thousand years. Chopin was Polish, as too was the world's first House of Parliament and many great thinkers and artists. Though I have and will never hold a Polish passport, I am Polish at my core; in a way only refugees can understand. The ancient battles and conflicts that make up the history of this star-crossed nation were again blazing at the time of my birth.

Two of the people caught in this thousand-year-old conflict were my parents. They would be intimately involved in the horrific events that made up the Polish reality of World War II. They were both exceptionally smart people and adept at their craft. They were spies. The war would not kill them but it would leave them broken inside.

This is the tale of the impact they had upon me and the determination it took to break away in my quest to go from a refugee camp to a penthouse. To get there, I broke through personal and professional taboos that at times left me hurt and vulnerable. There were days I thought I might never recover but in the end I did.

However, getting there was just the start of the story, for I was challenged time after time by circumstances that would pull me back down into the pit of despair. Anyone who wants proof that they can overcome crushing circumstances, no matter their age, will find it in this book. I hope it is of interest and benefit to those who read it. I have opened myself up and revealed secrets from parts of my past I have never wanted to share before.

History is only as good as the records we leave behind. This is the record of my life.

Acknowledgements

This book is about my life and I want to take a moment and thank everyone who has made it richer by his or her presence. In particular, there are a few people who I need to acknowledge by name.

My son Jonathan brought meaning to my life. He taught me what it is to truly love someone. Jonathan was there at the worst of times and helped me pull through. I love him unconditionally. I also am so thrilled with his wonderful wife, Aubrey. They are a tremendous team who make each other better.

My husband Donald Fuller is my partner in life. He gives me so much joy. We love, we work and we travel the world together. My life has not been the same since the day he came into it. I love him passionately.

My brother Richard is a wonderful, responsible and mature man who I could not do without, now. I am so glad he has come back into my life. He's lived a rich and diverse life and shared portions of my life that allow him to understand me in ways others can't.

My sister, Ewunia, brought love and light to a family, that needed so much of both. I will always love her.

My business mentor Brian Kent is the first person who ever truly believed in me. He is the one who had the courage to make me the youngest and sole female executive in a 5,000-person corporation. Without knowing it, he was instrumental in building up the self-esteem of a young lady who was coming from nowhere.

A special thanks to Dan Burakowski, the man who became the "father figure" my son so desperately needed, at a crucial time in his life. He was there for both of us.

Ewa Olszewska has been my friend since I was 2 months old. To this day I love our "artistic" adventures as we travel the world visiting theaters, ruins and museums.

Andrea Stanton is a friend for life who has always been able to make me laugh (and sometimes scream). She is a wonderful travel companion and a special friend.

Johann Lippert, deserves a huge thank you for being willing to financially back a wanna-be real estate mogul, when no one else would. His help and faith will always be cherished.

George Milton is the man who introduced me to the fun side of Hollywood. I will always smile at the memories of our walks down the Red Carpet. His generosity in times of need will never be forgotten.

Lizzie Taylor, my God-Child, is a wonderful young lady, who I think of as the daughter I never had.

Phyllis Kaiser and I created our own "family" when we were both young single mothers. We had a blast doing it and I still laugh whenever I think about our years in La Jolla.

Marta Vereker is another friend with whom I travel the world, sometimes with her loving daughters Susie and Catherine. Our trips are treasured events on the calendar of my life.

Jolyon Wilde who helped convince me that commercial real estate was the place for someone with my background. He also happens to be the only person in real estate, other than myself, that I ever worked for.

Andrew Dutton-Parish is my wonderful and ever faithful escort to all of the balls, operas and ballets that Don is so grateful that he does not have to attend. We both thank you.

Last, but not least, I want to thank Kevin O'Donnell, without whom this book would never have been written. His patience and talent are greatly appreciated. Writing this book together has been a transformative experience and his insight has made it more than it otherwise would have been.

1

WE ALL COME FROM SOMEWHERE
(2010)

"Out of suffering emerge the strongest souls. The most massive characters are seared with scars. Suffering becomes beautiful when anyone bears great calamities with cheerfulness, not through insensibility but through greatness of mind." – Kahlil Gibran.

As I sit on a plane leaving London, I look down on the Atlantic far below. An opera plays in my earphones as I sip from a glass of water, topped with a wedge of lemon. I can clearly remember the first time I saw these dark gray waters. I was a four-year-old child, without a passport or a country, heading for a new life in a refugee camp in post World War II, England; the country that gave me my education and my start in life. I have long since moved to America, a land that I love passionately, but I keep a home in London and always shall.

This is the story of how I went from a refugee camp to a penthouse to the poorhouse and back again. Along the way I was shot at, kidnapped and betrayed. I'm a survivor who has survived being horribly wounded by cowardly men and enjoyed being boldly protected by caring men.

In my early years, I learned that life could be dark and dangerous. If you are lucky, there will be loved ones there for you when you most need them. I discovered though that the only person you can truly depend upon, is yourself. There were times that I thought I was going to die but in each case I pulled myself up by my bootstraps.

Because of business risks I took, at an age that many people are starting their retirement; I do as I wish. This book is for anyone who thinks it's too late or too hard to achieve his or her dreams.

I'm heading back to California to join the love of my life. He entered my world when I was fifty-two years old and had no intention of ever getting married again. I'm not afraid to say that I enjoy the way he looks at me. To this day, I wake up and work out hard. I keep my body in good shape and I do my best to look attractive. As I've grown older, I've grown no less passionate nor romantic. In my single days, while many women subscribed to the belief that sex was a sin, I was having a hell of a good time.

In the end, it is my relationships, with my son and my husband, that allow me to call my life a success. The secrets I have learned along the way have been well earned. I've ended up wealthy enough but I count my friends and family as the only true riches in my life - well except my jewelry. I admit it, I love my jewelry. Besides, a nice necklace helps, when one is dining with royalty or walking the red carpet at the Oscars. Who am I kidding? A nice necklace helps when you're eating oatmeal.

I believe that in order to know who you are, you need to know where you come from. In the next few chapters you will meet my parents and you will know where it is I come from.

2

My wish is that this book becomes an inspiration to some of those who read it. No one but you can tell yourself that you're too old to do something. No one but you can force yourself to give up on your dreams. No one but you can wake up and say; this is the day that I'm going to start a new adventure.

2

KAROLINA
(1939)

It was August 27, 1939, and my mother, a beautiful young Polish socialite named Karolina, was attending a party filled with cigar-smoking men in military uniforms. The smile on her beautiful face, and the rouge on her cheeks, was more than enough to turn any of them into an eager conversationalist.

To this point in her young life, Karolina had already collected six marriage proposals, all of which she had turned down. She was quite adept at playing a man's heartstrings, without letting him pluck hers.

A string quartet played in the background while the officers tried to turn Karolina's pretty head in their direction. She was happy to oblige, intent upon learning the latest plans of the tyrant, rattling his saber, next door in Germany. Adolf Hitler had been focusing his rhetoric in Poland's direction for months, and young Karolina Mickiewicz was on a mission to discover the Third Reich's true intentions.

KAROLINA

Karolina was a Polish beauty with dark hair and sultry looks. Her singing voice added to her allure and a Hollywood movie producer had tried to get her to come to America with him, a year before, only to be kicked out of the house by Karolina's outraged older sisters. Karolina's parents had died by the time she was 11, leaving their fourteen children behind. Karolina and her siblings had been raised by French governesses, who were strict disciplinarians.

Karolina had been taught to speak multiple languages, her manners were impeccable and she was a master of polite conversation. She was also a maverick who demanded she be taught how to shoot a gun, master the bow and arrow, pilot airplanes and ride horses. Karolina was a modern woman who dared to wear pants and refused to bow down to any man.

As times had grown turbulent, Karolina's unique talents were apparent to a number of high ranking officers and she was mobilized by the Polish army. She became an informant, or in more dramatic parlance; a spy. What Karolina and others had recently learned, was heart stopping. Hitler was coming. The only question was: when?

The Polish government was rapidly preparing for yet another battle to defend their borders. Karolina knew from her military sources that her friends, family and fellow countrymen stood little chance if they were attacked. Poland had been busy rebuilding its army; however, with scarce resources available, many of their soldiers were carrying weapons that would have been antiquated during World War 1. The Polish cavalry still had many of its men on horseback. Meanwhile, the Third Reich was lining up its new, state-of-the-art armor plated assault vehicles and tanks at the border.

On this particular night, Karolina found a particularly forthcoming German who whispered something into her ear. What he said turned Karolina's blood cold. The date was set, the invasion was coming. Hitler's army was about to break its twenty-year truce with Poland.

3

CAPTURED

Karolina rushed back to her office and immediately began burning papers that Hitler's officers would come looking for. She had records of troop movements and the names of officers that had to be protected. In this time, before digital cameras and instantaneous information, they would be looking for names and locations.

Four days later, on Sept. 1, 1939, Nazi troops stormed into Poland as Karolina raced out to meet a driver that had been ordered to take her to safety. Karolina tried to jump into the car, but she was thrown to the ground by a man who took the last open seat for himself.

Karolina rolled through the mud and came to rest in a ditch by the side of the road. She laid there through the night hiding, as the Nazi tanks, trucks and troops roared past her. The fighting was fast and fierce. The Poles fought with everything they had; they just didn't have enough.

The initial defeats were but a harbinger of what was to come. One third of the Polish people would be dead by the end of the war. Another third would leave their country and never make it back. Poland was stripped of two thirds of its population in five years. By design, a disproportionate number of those left would be from the less educated portion of the population. Hitler's troops were ordered to eliminate as many of Poland's business, political and cultural leaders as possible.

Five hundred German Concentration camps would be set up on Polish land, along with the majority of the infamous extermination camps. Hitler tried to hide many of his worst atrocities, from the general population of Germany, by keeping them in the occupied territories. The sins his regime would perpetrate in Poland were of the greatest magnitude and their ramifications linger to this day.

Karolina went by foot to the next village, where she was again charged with destroying any papers that could lead the Germans to members of the military and the resistance. For the next several weeks, she went from village to village, doing the same. Finally, she reached Krakow, where she joined the nascent underground resistance army that would eventually cover the entire country and grow to nearly half a million members.

Krakow has long been considered one of the most beautiful cities in Europe. While Warsaw would be nearly bombed into oblivion, the German officers were ordered to leave the beautiful plazas and churches of Krakow intact, as a prize for Hitler. The resistance movement established a foothold in these protected buildings, struggling to fight against impossible odds.

Once she made contact, Karolina shared a room in a 'safe' house, while gathering as much intelligence as she could seduce out of the invading soldiers, until finally her identity was compromised. With the Germans close on her heels, Karolina was spirited away in the middle of the night. She and six men, officers disguised as civilians, were put in a truck and driven towards the border. Once there, they would be on their own, until they made contact at a predetermined point with the exiled Polish Army in France.

As they neared their destination, Karolina began to breathe a bit easier. They were let out of the truck and started walking the final distance through the woods that bordered Czechoslovakia. At the crossing point, something was off. The hairs on Karolina's neck bristled. There were soldiers waiting for them and they were speaking Russian. Their guide suddenly disappeared, having betrayed them for naught but a few dollars. He had delivered them into the hands of their supposed ally, Stalin.

While the world watched with horror as Hitler's troops stormed into Poland from the West, Russian troops had undertaken their own invasion from the East. In direct defiance of the freshly signed Molotov-Ribbentrop pact, Russian troops were killing Poles just as effectively as the Germans.

Karolina could barely breathe as she and the others were herded, at gunpoint, into the back of a covered truck. Karolina sat there shaking. The back flap was dropped and everything went black.

RETREAT INTO SILENCE

Karolina rode in horrified silence before arriving at a prison camp, where she was immediately separated her companions before being thrown into a freezing cell. Every night, Karolina was dragged to an interrogation room. The Russians demanded she admit that the men with her were officers in the Polish Army.

The interrogators were also intent on getting the names of more members of the resistance, still out there hiding. They beat Karolina mercilessly but she would not speak. They would cock a pistol and put it to her temple; still they got nothing. Like so many of her countrymen, Karolina would die before she would betray her country.

During this entire time, Karolina's only communication with her fellow prisoners was via Morse code. She and the others would tap out messages on the metal pipes that went from cell to cell. Karolina was forced to sleep on the freezing cold cement floors without so much as a blanket. The conditions were unbearable; yet she endured.

The torture continued night after night and the bright light that had burned in Karolina's eyes, dimmed. Karolina found refuge in a quiet place, deep inside, where she alone could go. Finally, no one's screams, not even her own, could reach her. Realizing she would never speak, the interrogators eventually gave up. What remained of Karolina's body was trucked out to a POW camp, near Siberia, where she was to start serving the twenty-five year term she had been given.

Karolina woke each morning, so cold that she voluntarily stripped in front of ogling Russian guards and stood beneath an ice cold outdoor shower, just to get her blood moving again. Her system was in such shock that she could not even think of anything but surviving, one moment at a time. Time disappeared and omnipresent pain was all that registered in Karolina's mind.

Though barely able to walk, Karolina was forced to cut timber out of the frozen forest and haul it back to camp for the comfort of the robust Russians. Three times, Karolina was delivered to the morgue in anticipation of her death. Each time, however, she refused to die and was sent back to collapse on the cement floor that was her bed. At night Karolina would drift into an exhausted sleep, dreams of the parties and gaiety of her youth unable to penetrate the nightmare of her new reality. Violated in every way, Karolina was on the verge of death.

5

ZYGMUNT

Less than a year earlier, right when Karolina was eliciting information out of unwitting German businessmen, a young member of the Polish diplomatic corps, in Hamburg, Germany, was making a frantic call back to Warsaw. Outside, German soldiers had suddenly rolled up, in armored vehicles, and surrounded the consulate he was working in.

Young Zygmunt Renkawicz instantly ascertained the situation. He and the other members of the consulate had just become Hitler's first prisoners in the upcoming war. He knew that it would be just moments before the encircling soldiers would cut the phone lines. Zygmunt knew the importance of the message he had to get out. His life and the lives of his fellow diplomats, both there and in other cities, were at stake.

Zygmunt's family had a grand tradition of service. His father's life had been lost while following the direct orders of General Pilsudski, known as the World War I Liberator of Poland. Zygmunt was willing to suffer the same fate, now.

While the other diplomats stared out of the windows with trepidation, Zygmunt raced to his office and grabbed the phone on his desk. He dialed as fast as he could. There was a click at the other end of the line. Not waiting to hear a voice, he yelled out that the consulate was surrounded by Nazis. They were prisoners. A moment later the line went dead.

Though he did not know it at the time, Zygmunt's quick message had indeed been received. In Warsaw, the Polish government responded by instantly surrounding the German embassy and capturing their own hoard of diplomats. The first acts of open hostility had occurred and, for at least the moment, Poland was giving no quarter to the Nazis.

Poland, home to one of the three oldest Universities in Europe, had at many times been more advanced and powerful than their Germanic neighbors. However, 20th century military science had been embraced a few years sooner by those in Berlin than those in Warsaw, and the rest of Europe. Those few years might as well have been a thousand. Zygmunt had seen enough to know that militarily, Poland stood no chance. Politicians and diplomats were Poland's first, and last, line of defense.

While the Poles were trying to negotiate a prisoner exchange, the Gestapo transported the diplomats to a prison where they were interrogated, ruthlessly. Zygmunt was thrown down and beaten every time he refused to divulge the information they wanted. As a man who was prepared to die for his country, absorbing a beating was well within Zygmunt's capacity to endure; and he did. They got nothing from him. Finally, mostly due to Zygmunt's warning, an exchange of diplomatic personnel was agreed to.

Zygmunt, along with the entire consulate staff, was transported back to Poland. Zygmunt was immediately inducted, as a captain, into the Polish Army. He was placed in Intelligence and fought the invasions, first the Germans, then the Russians. One night, Zygmunt went to meet a contact and was instead met by the muzzle of a Russian gun and quickly scheduled for deportation to an unknown destination.

On the day Zygmunt was scheduled to be transported out of Poland, there was a mix-up. He was supposed to be on a train, along with 4,200 other officers, headed for a wooded area of Russia, known as Katyn. Due to a clerical error, another man, who was a soldier, not an officer, was mistakenly taken in his place. By the time the mistake was discovered, the train had left. Zygmunt was instead put on the soldier's train, headed for a prison camp.

By the time Zygmunt was less but halfway to his destination, the other train had reached the forest of Katyn. The 4,200 passengers were marched into the woods until they came to stop in a meadow. Each officer was handed a shovel and ordered to dig a long deep trench at gunpoint. When they finished, they were shot in the back and buried in the ditch.

Many of the men were still breathing as the dirt was shoveled onto them. The horror of their deaths would not be traced to the hands of the Russians until well after the war was over. In all, it is estimated that as many as 45,000 victims were buried in the graves of Katyn and the surrounding area.

Not all of the dead bodies belonged to members of the military; many belonged to doctors, lawyers, teachers, landowners and writers. Any educated Pole was a target. Back on the train, Zygmunt, not knowing the bullet he had just dodged, looked out through cracks in the wood, at the sparse and stark terrain that so perfectly matched his mood.

6

PRISON CAMP

Before he was placed in the general population, Zygmunt was held in a cell where he was nearly beaten to death by some Russian soldiers. He survived the savage attack and was eventually put in the yard of the Ulbroka prison camp. Once there, Zygmunt's utility with languages was put to use. He was forced to teach Russian officers how to speak German and English.

As much as he loathed those he taught, his work gave him access to valuable information and news. When Zygmunt first heard that Hitler had attacked Russia he anticipated what would happen next and positioned himself accordingly. As a studied historian, Zygmunt knew that Hitler would inevitably attack Russia and when he did, Stalin would want the Poles on his side.

General Sikorski, president in exile of the Polish government, had been agitating Stalin for the release of his soldiers. After Hitler broke their alliance, Stalin did indeed realize that he could use Sikorski's help against the Nazis. Sikorski had one condition, his soldiers would gladly battle the Nazi's but only at the side of the Western Allies and not the Russians, whom they did not trust.

Stalin agreed and allowed a first wave of Poles out of his prison camps. A short time later, he would reverse his decision, but in the interim thousands of prisoners were released. They were organized into military units and set off on a dangerous journey to join the Allied forces in the Middle East. Two of the people starting the trek had been released after two helatious years in captivity, one was Zygmunt and the other was Karolina.

7

THE TREK BEGINS

During the ensuing months, polish patriots died by the hundreds. At times they were stranded on trains that lacked everything from coal to conductors. Men and women would go off to scour for food and come back to an empty track, left to fend for themselves in a frozen land of foreign foes. Food was always scarce and in many cases nonexistent. When there was no train available, they fought through snowdrifts in carts, and on foot, for days at a time. Along the way, as hard as the conditions were, Karolina's spirit began to revive and along with it, her physical beauty.

With Nazi troops occupying Western Europe, the Polish troops went east and then south on a nine-month journey that would eventually take them into Persia. Once there, they would merge with a larger Polish force being led by General Wladyslaw Anders. From there they would be dispersed to fight in almost every sector of the war. The transient army that Karolina and Zygmunt were in, was led by General Michal Tokarzewski.

On their path to the Middle East, Tokarzewski's troops had few weapons to protect themselves but their most dangerous enemy was the Siberian winter. At times, every step became a frozen nightmare. Any joy that one could find along the way had to be taken quickly. As they traveled, Poles who had been released from civilian prison camps, would join if they were capable of walking. Those that were too weak, had to be left behind; most likely to die.

As he made his way south with his new army, the General's gaze fell upon the lovely features of Karolina. He soon began to lavish her with attention, and propositions, that the well bred Karolina found inappropriate. Even after the horrors she had been through, Karolina held on to her virtue. While she had been a well-known socialite prior to the war, her love was not for sale. She found the married General's behavior boorish. She was a young lady and he was an old scoundrel.

The General responded in true scoundrel form by placing Karolina under 'house' arrest. It was rather obvious why he did so when it turned out that the 'tent' she was assigned to was right next to the General's. Finally, partly as a ploy to fend off his advances, Karolina opened herself up to the attention of men, less rude and far less married.

One of these men was a debonair spy with a brilliant mind and dashing good looks. Zygmunt had blond hair and blue eyes that smoldered with a deep brooding intelligence. He found the brunette Karolina's beauty captivating and she found him intriguing. The two of them began to have conversations that grew more intimate as their trek carried on. They shared a love of language and of diplomacy. Before the army was out of Siberia, three men proposed to Karolina. Zygmunt was the one to whom her answer was "yes".

THE WEDDING MARCH

Though she found Zygmunt alluring, Karolina did not marry him for love; her heart had been won by another. However, the man she did love had a wife whose fate was unknown. During these desperate times, numerous men and women moved on from their pre-war marriages but Karolina would not be party to such a move. Though it grieved her greatly, Karolina turned her back on the man she loved and said "yes" to the man she found intriguing, Zygmunt.

Their wedding took place in the midst of a white frozen landscape with an army coat serving as Karolina's gown. Zygmunt looked dashing. In the midst of the madness this was a moment that made them all civilized again. After two years of horror, Karolina again found the strength to smile. A military priest pronounced them husband and wife and the celebration began. As simple as the ceremony was, the reception was of magnificent proportion.

The night before their wedding, a truck had arrived from Moscow, compliments of General Tokarzewski. Karolina's marriage had more amused than upset the General and he had sent for barrels of vodka, in order to celebrate. As soon as the Priest pronounced Zygmunt and Karolina married, the general ordered his men to begin drinking. As good soldiers will do, the men followed their orders and they drank; and they drank; and they drank.

For three days, time stood still in the middle of a snowy wonderland. Then the barrels were empty, the war beckoned and their wretched journey continued. In the course of their trek, both Karolina and Zygmunt would contract typhoid. Unlike many others, they would survive. The way they did so, would later be seen as the first symptom of the sickness that would infect their marriage.

Karolina's twenty-four hour a day vigilance most definitely prevented Zygmunt from dying. She stayed by his side, changing his sheets, as they became drenched, by the sweat one exudes when struck by typhoid. However, when Karolina succumbed to the same sickness, Zygmunt put her in a makeshift medical tent and left her fate solely in the hands of the overworked medical staff.

Once Karolina was strong enough to travel, she and Zygmunt were dispersed to the Palestinian territory. There, they and much of the rest of the army rested while they awaited their orders. Despite the arduous nature of their journey, Karolina was slowly coming back to life. Indeed, by the end of their trek a child was growing within her body.

Shortly after arriving, and before she and Zygmunt could even contemplate their future child, the troops were shipped out. Zygmunt was sent, along with others from the intelligence unit to Italy, where he would infiltrate high governmental society as a spy.

Karolina and five other pregnant women remained in the city of Tel Aviv, to have their babies. On September 23, 1943, my mother gave birth to a young girl named Barbara Elzbieta Zofia Maria Prawdzic-Witoslawska, or Basia, as I would come to be known.

I would never know the pain and torture my parents suffered in Siberia, yet the lingering effects of their wounds would affect me greatly for years to come.

9

PALESTINE
(1943)

My mother's ravaged body was barely able to deliver me into this world. I then almost died before they discovered that my mother's milk was poison. I was fed by an Arab wet nurse who helped me regain my strength. Like my mother, I too suffered from a terrible bout of typhoid that almost proved fatal. By the time I would leave the Middle East, I would know the local doctors well.

The worst medical emergency I faced had nothing to do with an illness. When I was almost three years old, after we had moved to Jerusalem, I got hold of a box of matches. While I was sitting alone, I lit a match and set my dress on fire. My mother rushed into the room and threw a blanket on top of me. However, a full pack of matches had been clenched tightly in my hand. The resulting phosphorous burn required immediate attention. The local hospital was anything but sanitary and a nurse succeeded in infecting the wound.

A few days later, my mother took off the bandages to discover that the infection had spread horrifically. My hand was swollen to twice its size. When we returned to the hospital, the doctor told my mother that it was so advanced that the only thing to do, was to amputate the arm, just below the shoulder. The doctor reached for his saw as my mother grabbed me and ran out of the room.

She raced all the way to the home of a Jewish doctor she knew. He had told her of a new medicine, called penicillin, which was working wonders. It was only available, at that time, to military doctors, but he had managed to get hold of some through the back door.

It was the Sabbath, and in order to get to him, my mother had to climb over a security wall and sneak up to his back door. He answered her frantic knocks, took one look at my arm, and pulled us inside. He immediately began administering doses of the contraband penicillin. To my mother's great relief, the medicine worked, stopping the infection, and thus saving my arm.

In Jerusalem we had a room in a home where a number of Polish women were living. These women shared my mother's joy of freedom and the belief that they would soon be returning to their homeland. One of the other women there had a daughter, named Ewa Olszewska. It was there in the world's most conflicted and sacred city that my first memories were formed, and Ewa, born but two months after me, was a part of most of them. Our mother's became best friends and we became inseparable. To this day, Ewa holds a special place in my life.

Aside from my multiple bouts with illness and self-afflicted medical emergencies, my first impressions of life were happy and bright. I was in a city, however, whose future was dark and foreboding. As the war was ending, the British government was trying to extricate itself from the one part of the world that wanted to keep on fighting.

Palestine was a British Mandate, but it was not part of the British Empire. This meant that I was not a British subject and thus was given no passport. This also meant that the exhausted British forces were anxious to extricate themselves from the brewing battles that were bubbling up all around them.

Jews were leaving Europe by the thousands and streaming into Palestine, where they demanded a nation of their own. The Arab population was in violent opposition to any solution that resulted in a Jewish state being formed on the land they and their families had occupied for thousands of years. Eventually, Britain turned the problem over to the nascent UN. As the rest of the world decided the political fate of Palestine; the inhabitants fought.

I still remember the booming thunder that accompanied the frequent gun battles. After the Yalta conference, in 1945, sirens split the air at an ever increasing pace, sending us running for the nearest shelter. In the rest of the world, the war had ended, while in Palestine, it was just beginning. The new nation of Israel was being carved out of the ancient land that surrounded us and all hell was breaking loose.

When I was born, Jerusalem was filled with Jews, Muslims, Catholics and others of numerous ancient beliefs. Left alone, Jerusalem was fully capable of handling its own affairs but with its population nearly doubling overnight, it split apart along ethnic lines.

10

JERUSALEM

Though Jerusalem was exploding, the politics of hate were for adults; as a young girl, I loved my city. I would return to Jerusalem, much later in life, on two occasions, and in each case I was again touched by the mystic powers of its ancient walls. During my first years there, I adored my numerous Jewish and Arabic friends and they adored me; hopefully, not just for the beautiful Italian dolls my father sent me for my birthdays. I was only too happy to give them away, not realizing they were worth a relative fortune.

To this day, I have little trouble parting with material goods. I love the utility that money brings: the access to wonderful new places; the friends that one meets on expeditions and the ability to more easily create new entrepreneurial adventures. The accumulation of material goods, however, is something I can do without - except of course for the jewelry. Ladies, I admit it: in my later years I have come to love good jewelry.

The Jerusalem that I lived in was always exciting. I remember the sun shining down on colorful buildings that housed an eclectic collection of people from around the world. I thought the sandy streets were there simply for my benefit. My friends and I felt like we could follow them forever.

After her time in hell, my mother reveled in her newfound freedom. She was still painfully thin and in need of rest, but Karolina was coming back to life. My mother loved to sit with the other women and talk about the future that once again looked promising. They planned for the days after the war, when they would return to Poland and help rebuild the country they so loved.

When my mother would sit down to kibitz, I would run out to play. I was born with an independent streak and I had no fear of making my own way through the bustling boulevards and narrow alleys that surrounded my home. The air was filled with calls to prayer, merchants hocking their wares and of mothers calling their children home for dinner. I understood the words I heard and my place in this chaotic and charismatic place.

My first language was indeed Arabic, which I learned from our landlady and my friends in the streets. In the family tradition, I would move on to speak Polish, English, French and when I came to California years later, a bit of Spanish.

There were moments of great joy when my mother and I would walk hand in hand through the streets. We'd walk to the primitive Jerusalem zoo and spend hours wandering through its confines. I loved that place. I remember one day standing at the monkey cage watching as the dominant male continuously ripped the food out of a female monkey's hands. Later in life, I would reflect back on this and find in it parallels to the behavior of some of the men I ended up dealing with.

When it was time to leave the zoo, we'd walk home through the crowds. My mother would throw her head back and sing with a voice so beautiful; I can hear it to this day. I loved Jerusalem and during our four magical years there, my mother and I formed a bond that would never be broken, at least not completely.

11

A FAMILY BETRAYED
(1945)

As the war drew to a close my father's predilection for languages, pretty women, and the halls of learning had led him to a privileged social circle in Rome. When he wasn't conversing with the elite, he was in the shadows, interrogating prisoners for the British. One night he walked into a room where a young Jewish freedom fighter was tied to a chair.

The prisoner's name was Menachem Begin, a fellow Pole, who had deserted General Ander's army to become a leader of the Jewish rebels known as the Irgun. Members of the Irgun were intent on creating a homeland for the Holocaust victims, by any means necessary.

In the waning days of the war the Irgun was becoming more trouble than the retreating Germans and Italians. Its bombings and clandestine attacks, in Palestine, were beginning to cause chaos. The British wanted to stop the Irgun and they suspected Menachem Begin of being one of the movement's key leaders.

Zygmunt started his interrogation and soon realized he was not dealing with a normal man.

A foe of such intellect and strength was seldom encountered. Zygmunt was exhilarated by their exchange. Begin would admit nothing but he expounded a series of views and values that Zygmunt agreed with. This future Prime Minister of Israel and Nobel Peace Prize winner walked out of the room and disappeared, my father knowing full well that he was guilty of the offenses the British suspected him of.

Though many of my father's faults would eventually cause me great personal pain, he intuitively believed in the equality of all men. Those born to pleasures and power had no more inherent right to the wealth of a nation than its poorest citizens, no matter their ethnicity. Zygmunt would spend endless energy in the future, fighting for the rights of refugees and victims of industrial oppression. Ironically, the only people he would have no time, nor concern for, would end up being those of his own family.

During his time as an interrogator, Menachem Begin would not be the only Jewish fighter my father let slip through England's net. Because of my father's predilection for freedom fighters, certain members of allied intelligence were deeply suspicious of him, but by definition, shouldn't everyone be suspicious of a spy?

When Zygmunt wasn't prying into the minds of prisoners, and spying on Mussolini's minions, he was loosening the corsets of a certain young countess. Their relationship blossomed and grand dreams were shared. Three years after I was born, the spark of life that had been rekindled in Karolina, first on her wedding day and subsequently in Jerusalem, was doused by a cold splash of reality. It was delivered in the guise of a letter.

Zygmunt wrote that he had found a new focus for his attention and affection. He wanted no more of the little family he'd left behind in the Promised Land. Zygmunt demanded a prompt Catholic annulment from Karolina. Their marriage was over. His words, so perfectly penned on fine linen paper, immediately set my mother on a determined course of action that Zygmunt would soon regret.

The horrors of war and men had stripped Karolina of all pretenses of joy; there was no indignity she had not suffered; yet the thought of her husband daring to throw her and their daughter away was too much. Every one of Karolina's brothers had died in the war along with all but two of her sisters. Theirs was a proud and prestigious family, and Karolina would not be humiliated within the circle of Polish women who, like her, were waiting in Palestine. Determined to keep her last shred of honor in tact, Karolina got a message to her one ally.

The General, still enamored with Karolina, ordered Zygmunt to England, where a portion of the Polish Army was taking up residence in various refugee camps, spread across the country. The one we were assigned to was in Foxley, 100 miles northwest of London. Zygmunt was to report there and wait for his family to join him. Zygmunt was furious and would resent Karolina for the rest of his life for stealing the glorious future that lay within his grasp. But a patriot to the end, he reluctantly followed orders and left his Countess behind.

Soon thereafter, I was holding my mother's hand, as we boarded a military transport ship, the MV Cheshire, bound for Portsmouth, England. We were the two of the few civilians on board but the soldiers were happy to have a four-year-old ball of fury running around and reminding them of why they had been fighting.

On the way out of the harbor, we passed an English warship that had been sent to help quell the attacks that were tearing Palestine apart. Little did I know that on that ship was a sixteen year old midshipman who would continue to cross paths with me until a day far in my future. On that day, our eyes would connect and our souls would be united.

On this day, however, all I could do was stare with open-mouthed awe at the size of the ship and the uniformed men standing on the deck, insuring my safety, as we left the most dangerous harbor in the world.

12

REFUGEES
(1947)

As a little girl of four, who had no idea what her father looked like, I was understandably confused when we entered the harbor of Portsmouth, England, on July 14, 1947. We anchored off shore and a boat filled with inspectors came to do a walk through, prior to allowing us to dock. They placed a shaky plank between the two ships and, thinking my father was on it, I pulled out of my mother's grip and raced down the narrow board, to the horror of everyone watching.

Unaware I had done anything wrong; I made it across and threw myself at the first uniformed man I saw. I yelled out in Arabic, "Daddy! Daddy!", only to be pulled off of the unknown soldier who, in perfect British fashion, remained at attention through my entire mugging. I was returned to my relieved, angry and embarrassed mother as the inspection began.

Finally, after we docked, my father walked up, gave a sullen nod of his head to my mother and turned, indicating we should follow. Confused, I grabbed my mother's hand and we marched behind the silent captain, who seemed to have no interest in us, whatsoever. Not knowing what was happening, I kept calling out to my father. But he ignored me. We soon boarded a military transport truck and eventually made it to a large, muddy camp filled with Quonset huts.

As opposed to the bright streets of Jerusalem, I was suddenly living in a world of grays and browns. Rain and clouds were far more common than the sunshine and blue skies I was used to. We shared one of the nondescript huts with another family. There was no bathroom or kitchen, just one room with a couple of cots, on a cement floor, and a thin wall that separated us from the family on the other side.

Our hut faced a forest and at night, when my mother left to visit neighbors, I'd lay there petrified, as the unfamiliar hoots and howls of the forest cascaded down upon me. My father was almost never home, during my childhood. His work kept him on the road almost 90% of the time.

Ever the patriot, Zygmunt had found a new cause which he could throw his energy and intellect into; the Polish trade union. He spent his time away from our home, fighting for the rights of immigrant Polish workers. Zygmunt's cause was far more noble than Zygmunt the man.

When he was home, I tried to spend as much time as I could outside, where it was quiet. My father's preferred form of communication was yelling, and my mother fought back in equally angry but far quieter tones. Her decorum allowed for hate but not for volume. I remember being in the middle of horrible fights that never seemed to end.

My father would grab my arms and shake me; demanding that I agree that he was right. Though he would scare me, my independent streak, and loyalty towards my mother, prevented me from doing as he demanded. I would stare at him, stubbornly refusing to speak until he would throw his hands up and storm out.

It was obvious that my father would never forgive my mother for dragging him away from Italy. I was but an extension of the woman who had denied him a glorious life. Slowly but surely, my mother's songs drifted away and over the course of the ensuing years, I watched her lose whatever joy had been rekindled in her soul.

The Arabic and Hebrew languages of Jerusalem were replaced predominantly by Polish and a small amount of English. My childhood was spent in a hybrid world where the adults tried to keep Polish customs alive. I had free range of this place, to the point that I actually changed pre-schools without my mother's knowledge. I had been going there for months before the school authorities discovered what I had done. They sent me back to the correct school, and I did it again. This time, they threw their hands up in the air and allowed me to stay in the school I preferred.

Everyone in the camp believed that they'd soon be heading home to Poland, a belief that would take decades to die. Thus, they had no desire to assimilate into the cities that surrounded them. Our camp was as Polish as the streets of Krakow. However, as Stalin brought down his 'Iron Curtain', the hopes of returning were extinguished and over time, the families in the camp began leaving for new lives in their new land.

13

MOVING ON... DOWN

The Polish refugees in our camp were citizens of no country; officially categorized as displaced people and political refugees. I had no passport; I was the citizen of no country. Poland had been handed to the Russians, at the Yalta Conference, making it impossible for most of the refugees to ever return to their homeland. If they did so, they would most likely be imprisoned.

Even if they could return, life behind the Iron Curtain was miserable. All rights were effectively taken away from the citizens living under Stalin's rule. Food in England was not plentiful, but in places such as Poland it was virtually nonexistent. As soon as crops were harvested, all but a small portion were loaded onto trucks and trains and sent to Russia.

Though most of the Polish refugees were highly educated; they were consigned to menial jobs due to their lack of English. Inevitably, there were British gentlemen more than ready to exploit this new source of desperately poor labor. The Poles were paid wages far below those of English workers and if they complained they found their families going without food the next day. This offended my father's honor, especially knowing the sacrifices the Poles made in the war. For example, in the great aerial Battle of Britain, one out of ten German bombers that were destroyed came down at the hands of a Polish pilot. Such sacrifice deserved better than the subhuman wages being offered.

My father threw himself into this new cause: hook, line and sinker. Simultaneously, his relationship with my mother could sink no lower. They settled into a 'cold war' of their own that was only broken by intermittent battles that left us all emotionally bloodied. The Karolina I had known in Jerusalem, disappeared before my young eyes.

To many Poles, my father was a hero. To the two people who lived under his control, he was a tyrant. He made every important decision and controlled the meager amounts of money that we lived upon.

After a year in our hut, we moved to the city of Cardiff, where we lived in a small room in a home filled with other families like ours. Every room was filled with people more concerned with survival than furnishings. For the first time I was put in an English school. I had no idea what anyone was saying, as Polish was the only language spoken at home. Within the year, however, I was speaking like a native.

When we lived in Cardiff, my mother gave birth to my sister, Ewunia. She was born with Down's syndrome and a more gentle soul has ever graced this planet. She would grow to be the only consistently loving part of our family. Though even Zygmunt could not completely ignore my sister's wondrous spirit, her condition only served to deepen my father's anger at being trapped in a family he wanted nothing to do with.

Soon after Ewunia's birth my mother received a telegram from some relatives who had gone to America prior to World War I. They had managed to acquire an amount of personal wealth and in an act of great kindness; they sent Karolina money to buy a small house.

My mother was thrilled, until Zygmunt took the money and used it to buy a house for the Polish trade union. Instead of Karolina having her own home with a little garden in the back, Zygmunt opened the local headquarters of the Polish trade union. My mother's protests were swept aside, as if they were nothing. Adding insult to injury, my father brought four young Polish students into the house. While they studied for the courses they attended at a nearby University, my mother was forced to clean and cook for them.

Karolina had been raised with servants who had done all of the housework for her and her siblings. In our home I became her servant. My loving mother had been replaced by a physically and emotionally exhausted master. Other than cooking our meager meals, which she consistently burned, I did all the cleaning, laundry and housework. My life became an endless succession of chores and school. The Karolina I had played with, and loved, was gone. There were no more hugs or songs, only suds and brushes.

Zygmunt continued to travel throughout England, organizing the Polish workers. In exchange for his endless work he received a small stipend that forced us to stay on welfare in order to survive. Potatoes were served ad nausea and dessert was an infrequent and tiny taste of sugar.

In early 1951, at the age of 7, we moved to London, and were assigned to the basement of another trade union building. It was five stories tall, with every single room in the building filled with wretchedly poor people like us. The sole bathtub was on the top floor, five flights up. There were no other children in the entire building, but I met a girl, named Hillary, who lived across the street and she became my first British friend.

My father was home a bit more now that we were in London. When he and my mother weren't fighting, he locked himself away, in a tiny closet under the staircase. He spent his time there reading immense books about history. At other times he would listen for news from Eastern Europe on his short wave radio. He would then pass what he learned on to Radio Free Europe.

At this point in his life, Zygmunt had lost all pretenses of his faith and was an avowed atheist. He withdrew into a silent world that had no room for his wife or daughters. I was old enough now to know that my mother's life was void of joy. I made a vow to myself to never end up like her. One way or another I would grow up and be in charge of my own life, free from tyrants of any type.

14

BANISHED
(1952)

A year later, my mother became pregnant. She eventually went to the hospital and came back with my little brother, Richard. However, I wasn't there to greet him. Even though I was doing an inordinate amount of the work at home, I still required resources, such as food and space in which to sleep; both of which were in short supply. Though the labor union paid my father a minuscule amount of money, they did value his efforts. The union offered to pay for boarding school if my parents wished to ship me out of the house. The union did not have to offer twice. Shortly before my ninth birthday I was sent away.

As dreary and dysfunctional as my home was, it was still my home. On top of that, I was being shipped out in exchange for a new sibling. This was horribly disconcerting to my psyche. My form of protest was to completely cut off any communication with my parents. This disturbed Karolina, but Zygmunt didn't even notice.

For the next three years, I would move away and only see my parents a few times a year. Being in a new environment could have been a blessing. I could have been sent to a school filled with loving spiritual teachers; but I wasn't.

15

LOSING MY RELIGION

To this day it shocks me to think that my parents could so blithely ship their eight-year-old child off to a school they knew almost nothing about. The boarding school was a dark and dreary place run by Roman Catholic nuns who taught the New Testament, while ruling over their students with Old Testament techniques. The school was isolated in a converted walled estate, miles away from the city. It was there, in the confines of the church, that I lost my belief in organized religion.

Slaps, detentions and cross comments were the currency in which the nuns traded. They would slap us with nettles or make us kneel on gravel for hours at a time if we dared crossed them. Many of the women that had taken their vows of celibacy, before and during the war, had done so in order to escape hard times. At my new school, those who wore the 'habit' because of their love for others were few and far between.

During this nearly four-year period of my life I felt alone and unloved. I would only be allowed home for two weeks at Christmas and two weeks at Easter. During the summers, I was

41

sent to a Polish scouting camp. I became isolated during these years. My best friends became my books and my lifelong love affair with reading began.

At night, I would sit in my bed and read the works of classic authors such as Dickens. Then, when the lights went out I would recite the stories to the other girls in our dormitory. Sometimes I would make stories up on the spot, spinning my own scenarios. Once the other girls fell asleep I would continue to read, beneath the covers, with the aid of a flashlight.

The nuns did their best to keep me from even this pleasure, but I could usually hear them coming, in time to douse my light and feign sleep. Though I loved reading, I despised my classes. This had more to do with the teachers than the subject matter. The nuns seemed to be conspiring to banish any happiness from my soul.

I was not the only one who suffered. One day I awoke to the sounds of nuns storming through the hallways. Three older girls, who had failed in an earlier attempt to escape, had literally tied their sheets together and scaled down the walls to the ground below. They had made their getaway just after lights out the night before and raced off into the night. That whole day we spoke of nothing else and hoped they would succeed in their quest for freedom.

Instead, they were caught and brought back by the police. The Mother Superior was incensed. For three weeks she locked the girls in a room where they were served only one meal a day. One day I saw the parents of one of the girls who were being given the run-around. When the nuns weren't looking, I told the woman that her daughter was locked up, in a room upstairs.

The school was a place right out of the Dickens novels I was reading. A "field trip" was composed of a week spent in fields digging up potatoes that would be served back to us in the form of bland mash. Things were so bad that I faked horrible toothaches in order to get out of school. The dentist's drills were blunt and there was no anesthesia and I still preferred his office to the nuns' classrooms. To this day, I have four needless fillings in my teeth.

The independent streak I first exhibited as a pre-schooler, in the refugee camp, only grew stronger now as the nuns came at me with their dark dogma. No matter how often the nuns punished me, I refused to accept their pretense that I was inherently evil and it incensed them. I skipped mass on an almost constant basis. Though they sent search parties out for me they never caught me in the act. They did however; take to sending two older girls to escort me to confession every Saturday. I retaliated by relaying a consistent series of fictional sins I kept on retainer, in my mind.

Eventually, another girl and I ran away. Like the three before us, we too were back within a day and punished severely. Things truly came to a head, however, when I forgot to kiss the hand of one of the most notorious nuns in the school, Sister Victoria.

We were expected to kiss the nuns hands whenever we saw them, this included when we entered and departed class. I'd rushed in late one day and forgotten to kiss Sister Victoria's outstretched hand. She called me to the front of the class and asked me if I knew what I had done.

In all honesty, I had no idea what she was talking about. She sent me into the hall to think about it. She called me back in and asked if I'd remembered. By now, it dawned on me what she was talking about but I was not about to give in to her petty vindictiveness.

Even though I was emotionally beaten down by my father, my thoughts were my own. Sister Victoria could order me all she wanted, I was not about to do what she told me to. I feigned ignorance and she sent me back to the hall. She called me in again and this time she realized that I was simply being obstinate. She sent me into the hall once more, following me through the door, with a ruler in her hand. The rage inside her took over and she hit me across the face with it, three times, as hard as she could.

Though the pain was excruciating, I just stared at her red fuming face, still refusing to kiss her hand. She seemed to realize she had crossed the line. She spun around and went back into class. Tears welled in my eyes, but I wiped them away. I collected myself and followed her. I only told one friend what had happened, refusing to acknowledge that the nun could hurt me in any way that mattered. However, my face was still marked two weeks later when my mother miraculously showed up out of the blue.

I was so bitter about my circumstances that I refused to come down and see her. The friend who I had told about the beating went instead. She told my mother what the nun had done to me. Karolina was incensed and sprang into action.

My mother was not about to let anyone but family treat her daughter harshly. She marched into the office of the head mistress and demanded that they punish the offending nun. Compared to Russian interrogators the nuns were putty in her hands and shortly thereafter, Sister Victoria was banished to an isolated convent. At the end of the term, I was finally allowed to come back home.

16

THE NEW SCHOOL
(1955)

It turned out that my mother's reasons for bringing me home were more pragmatic than loving. Karolina was ill and needed her servant back. I again settled into a cold life filled with shouts and endless chores. Aside from my mother and father I was now also cleaning up after, and caring for, two little children.

Prior to leaving the boarding school I had sat for the national exams which, in those days, determined the quality of school a student may attend. I received very high marks, and was eligible to apply to any of the most prestigious schools in London. I settled upon a school, Sacred Heart, that was a forty-five minute train ride away from my parent's new flat.

Though Sacred Heart was run by nuns, just like my boarding school, the similarity ended there. The school's high rating was not handed out lightly. The nuns at Sacred Heart were strict, but they were fair and I was happy there. Part of my happiness was due to a young spirited girl, named Frances Treanor, who would become a dear friend.

Frances was a strong willed artist from a family of Irish descent. I recognized in her a kindred spirit as I too loved to draw. We bonded at a core level. Frances would go on to become a highly-respected painter and someone I would always be thankful for having in my life; even when our stubborn personalities clashed.

I had always been a tomboy and at Sacred Heart my athletic abilities started to draw attention. My father had been in the 1932 Olympics, competing in the modern pentathlon. Meanwhile, my mother had been as active as a young lady, of her day, could be. From the day I stepped inside the halls of Sacred Heart I was the top athlete in my class.

For a child who had always been told she was worthless, the attention I began to receive for my athletic prowess was a new and wonderful experience. For the first time in my life, I knew what it was like to be encouraged. Slowly but surely, I developed my own unique personality and social circle.

Sacred Heart was a traditional British institution that excelled at preparing its students for the top universities. The nuns would tell us openly not to speak with the help because we were being raised to a higher standard. Having started my life in a refugee camp I considered such notions as pure rubbish and ignored their admonitions.

At Sacred Heart, unlike my last school, I wanted to do well in class. I wanted to please my teachers and down deep I still wanted to please my parents. The first goal I accomplished; the last would prove to be impossible.

17

BETRAYAL

Shortly after I started at Sacred Heart, my mother's illness grew worse. An operation was scheduled and she went to a hospital to have a hysterectomy. After the surgery, a nurse inadvertently spilled a bowl of boiling water on my mother's scar and her recovery was set back. She was sent to a convalescent home for three months and my siblings and I were sent away as well.

Zygmunt had not cared for his new bride when she had suffered from typhoid, so there was not a chance that he would take care of his children while she was away. I stayed with my dear friend Ewa, whose family had also come to England after the war. I found her family to be a welcome change from my own dysfunctional home. Every Friday I would return to our house and spend hours cleaning up after my father. One day my father came home early and found me cleaning his bedroom.

I had been sent away a child and returned a barely budding teenager. There had been a few times, since my return, that I had caught my father staring at me with a look on his face I'd never seen before. On this day, he laid down on the bed and then completely uncharacteristically told me to do the same. I had no idea why and I was confused as I lay down next to him.

Moments later my world exploded as my father's hands were suddenly upon me. He proceeded to betray me in a way that no child should ever have to know. I took the train to Ewa's home that night, in a daze, unable to come to grips with what had just happened. Zygmunt had always been verbally abusive, but what he had just done was something I could never have expected, even from him.

I could not sleep that night, nor the next or the next. To this day I take a sleeping pill to help me overcome the insomnia that has plagued me ever since. I already suffered from recurring nightmares that had begun plaguing me shortly after we left war torn Jerusalem. In one, I walked a colorful narrow street filled with exotic sculptures. At the end was a gate. When I touched it, a bull would storm out at me. Another was in black and white and was filled with the sounds and fury of a battle that always ended with me being buried alive. Now, a new nightmare exploded in my head, making sleep an elusive and scary occurrence.

When my mother had recovered, we all returned home. My mother and father would never again share a bed. The little life my mother may have had left inside her, before the hysterectomy, was gone. She was still a lady with fine manners, but beneath the surface she was back in the place where no one's screams could reach her, especially mine. I returned to my life as a servant, caring for my siblings and cleaning for a father who had turned my life into a nightmare.

From that night on, I lived in fear of his every late night footstep. I would live with this threat until I was physically strong enough to stop him, four years later. My mother either never knew or never wanted to know what her husband was doing in the other room while she slipped off into her nightly coma. I was alone with a predator that controlled my every move.

Any faith I had left, after the boarding school, was now completely exorcised from my soul. I knew that no loving God would ever allow the evil that I had personally seen and experienced.

Compounding the problem was the fact that my father was no longer traveling. The trade union had become riddled with politics and my father had become fed up with all the backstabbing. He took a job as an accountant for a large international shipping company. His skill with languages also made him the company interpreter.

While it was a horrible turn of events to have Zygmunt home all the time, there was one small benefit. Each year, his company would ship horses in, from around the world, for two large horse shows. My father became the official interpreter for the shows. Frances and I would tag along and get backstage access to these events. I loved watching the beautiful animals and sometimes their handsome riders.

We also got to sit in box seats. At one show, when intermission came, we stood up and walked down the aisle. In front of us people moved to the side and stood at attention as we walked by. We could not understand what all the fuss was about. We got to the bottom of the stairs and were suddenly pulled to either side. I turned around and realized that the royal family had been walking behind us the whole way.

Soon after I returned from boarding school I noticed mysterious packages appearing on our doorstep. It turned out that they were coming from a spy working for the communist government of

Poland. They wanted my father to return to his former profession and spy for the Soviet controlled regime; something he would never consent to. He had risked his life over and over to defeat communism and the thought of now aiding the Russian puppet masters was repulsive.

However, the work my father had done with the Polish labor movement and previously as a spy, made him attractive to those now in power and the man courted my father relentlessly for several months. Soon after the Polish spy made contact, my father got another visit, this one from a member of British intelligence.

They had been keeping tabs on the movements of the man who had approached my father. The Brits wanted my father to accept the offer from the Polish consulate and act as a double agent. At this point, my father decided he'd had enough of the spy business and rejected both offers, forthwith.

After that Zygmunt's attention moved to intellectual pursuits. Over the next dozen years he would read the greatest historical, philosophical and theological texts on the planet, in their original languages. In the end, his reading would lead him back to the Catholicism of his youth. His spiritual relationship with God, whatever it was, had no effect on the sins he would continue to inflict upon me for four years until I could finally beat him off of me for good.

18

SALVATION
(1959)

When I turned sixteen, Sundays became my salvation. I would put on one of my two hand-me-down dresses, leave the house on my own, and meet my friends at church. I did have three dresses but my father had destroyed one in a fit of rage. My friends would come out of mass and I'd be there to join them. We would go to coffee shops and scurry about London all day. Some of the older boys had access to cars and we would drive outside of London and visit the countryside. Only when the night had lost its allure would I go home.

It was during this time that I began to realize the true importance of my friends. They became my family and to this day I cherish my friends and refuse to ever take them for granted or to abandon them.

I was determined to enjoy the time I had away from my home and the more I did so, the more I grew as a person. Even so, my self-perception at the time was that I was indeed the homely, worthless and dumb girl my father had always told me I was. To drive his point home Zygmunt would go to no ends to humiliate me.

One incident that took place during this time is quite illustrative. As a young teenager, I still had a very small bust. In order to compensate, I had taken to padding my dresses. My father hated me showing any kind of physicality and would be furious when he'd catch me doing so. One day my mother had friends over. My father was seated with them when I walked into the room.

Before I could say a word my father noticed that my bosom was more prominent than normal. He immediately started berating me for coming in dressed like a floozy. A moment later he jumped up, reached into my dress and pulled the pads out in front of everyone. I fled the room in horror, wishing somehow I could get away from this horrid place. I became determined to find a life beyond the reach of my father.

I joined the Oscar Kolberg dance company when I was 16. This was my second go round with dance. When we were in the refugee camp, I had tried to take ballet classes from a prominent ballerina from Poland. She told my father that she thought I had a gift for dance and should be encouraged to pursue it on a serious level. He responded by pulling me out the next day.

The woman who ran the company I joined as a teenager was named Olga Zeromska. She was a talented choreographer, who saw something in me. Though I was untrained, she nurtured my natural gifts, and I soon became one of her featured soloists. I had to sneak out to our rehearsals and performances, knowing that my father would stop me from dancing, if he found out. My mother however, enjoyed the performances.

Ewa joined as well. We were the two youngest members of the troupe. Ewa would dance until, as a young bride, her male chauvinist husband found it unacceptable for another man to hold her, while she performed. Now that I had started again, I was not about to stop. When the music started, I would melt into it. Under Olga's tutelage, the raw talent I was born with, was developed, and with it, my self-confidence.

Though my father had control over much of my life I was more and more secretive about what I was doing. I no longer told him anything and he knew less and less about my life outside of his tiny corrupt kingdom. At home, I would put on classical music and play it at all hours, in an attempt to escape the poisonous words that continued to flow from his mouth. When I was alone in my room, I would give myself up to the music and dance for hours.

I would sneak out on weekends and entertain real crowds with traditional and modern dances. Dance came very natural to me and I was soon the lead soloist of the group. During the week, I had school to distract me. Though I was exhausted from an ongoing lack of sleep, I was able to play sports and socialize with an ever-growing circle of friends. I began to garner the attention of young men, and though I had no idea why, due to my naiveté and self-image, I was soon being pursued by a number of them.

19

BOY OH BOY
(1960)

I had never whispered a word to my mother, of what my father was doing to me, and I continued to remain silent. I kept the pain and anger inside. Late at night, I'd lie in bed listening to my father type in the room next door. He worked past midnight every evening, reading his books and typing his thesis papers. He had an old mechanical typewriter that was annoyingly loud. The constant tap, tap, tap was horrible to listen to. However, the worst sound of the night was the sound of the last tap. For what followed that, was much worse.

The flat we lived in was in a mews. In the days before cars, people used horses and carriages for transportation. They kept them in stables, or mews, built throughout the city. The stable workers lived in rooms built in a row, above the stables. We lived in one of these rows of rooms. In order to get to one end of the apartment from the other, you had to walk through every single room. My father had to pass through my room in order to get from his office to his bedroom. One night, he made one of his horrid stops in my room and I vowed it would be for the last time.

I was strong, I was insanely mad and I was finally mentally mature enough to know that only I could stop the beast that was my father. That night marked the end of his abusive visits. When he finally left, unsatisfied, I laid in bed, unsure of what would happen next. All I truly knew, was what would not happen.

With his physical perversions no longer being satisfied, my father's abuse transformed into even more vicious attacks upon my character. As boys began to pay attention to me, his verbal abuse became almost lethal. Out of the blue one day, a teenaged acquaintance of mine came to our mews and asked my father for my hand in marriage. I was stunned and my father was furious. He sent him away in disgrace and then called me a whore. Though the physical abuse was over, Zygmunt's verbal abuse were still roaring along.

Though the boys were consistently turned away, I continued the process of breaking away from my father's clutches. I took a job on Saturdays and my father allowed me to keep it, so long as I gave him most of my earnings. I did so and reveled in my first taste of financial freedom. Despite everything, I would continue to give my parents money until the day they died. I gave it to my mother out of love and eventually, to my father, out of principle.

At the age of 17, I was still immune to the gazes of my suitors, wanting nothing to do with anyone of the opposite sex. However, there was a tall, dark and much older man, named Nur, who I had a most unique relationship with. Though we were totally platonic, for about a year, he wooed me with limos and visits to exquisite clubs that I never knew existed.

My father never knew that Nur existed. I never met him at my home. I did eventually tell my mother, at Nur's request, and she absolutely adored this man; and he was a man. Nur was 37 years old, twenty years older than me. He was extraordinarily wealthy with a whole harem of highly-paid ladies ready to do his bidding.

Nur never pressed me for physical affection of any kind. He came from Pakistan and I was some type of wonder to him. Perhaps I had an alluring innocence, or maybe a hardened edge? He may have seen in me someone that needed a friend, or just a young plaything that looked wonderful on his arm.

Whatever it was that Nur saw in me, he was smitten, and over the next year he opened my eyes to a world I soon came to love. Coming from the lowest place one can imagine, I found the high life was for me. I became a regular at the Savoy Hotel and other five star establishments.

I went from dancing at charitable events to dancing in the trendiest clubs in London. Soon after we met, I gave into Nur's requests to meet my mother. He took her for tea and explained that he had no ill intent in mind for her daughter. He was gracious, he was kind, and my mother loved him.

At times, I would play games with Nur and make myself unavailable, which only seemed to make him want to be with me more. One day he called and asked me to go to lunch. I told him that I couldn't go because I was going to lunch with all the girls that I worked with. Immediately, he told me to bring them along. Minutes later, he pulled up in his limousine followed by a string of taxis. He took us to the Carlton Hotel where he spent a fortune on his troupe of teenagers. We were almost fired en masse when we returned, four hours later.

For a girl living in a converted horse stable, these were transformative excursions. I realized that an amazing life was possible. I loved our luncheons and the clubbing. Each time we went out, it gave me faith that more than Quonset huts and cruel circumstances were to always be my lot in life. Nur possessed an evolved global view that he expressed quite eloquently. He helped open my mind in many ways that allowed me to grow as a person.

Almost 20 years later I would cross paths with Nur again. This time as a mature woman, I would take Nur to my bed for a beautiful and treasured night. However, when I was a vulnerable teenager, Nur never abused my trust and played a special role in an otherwise dark chapter in my life.

Though my father's sins were no longer met with anything short of fury, the damage was there to be seen by the trained eye, but only if someone was looking. In those times, such matters were swept under the rug and considered family business. I did however, plead with Karolina to leave Zygmunt and claim whatever happiness she could still have.

No matter how much I begged, Karolina refused to consider leaving the man who had in turn treated her like a slave and then as a nonexistent entity. In the end, Karolina chose false honor over true happiness. There was nothing I could do to help my mother, but I could change my own destiny. I vowed that I would break away and find happiness. I would find a way out.

20

THE BEGINNING OF THE BREAK
(1961)

Our family lived in modern London, but my parents existed within a micro-community of Polish refugees who clung to the ways of pre-war Poland. There were Polish libraries, Polish Universities, Polish Scouting Programs, Polish restaurants and Polish stores spread throughout London. Even though I was on the one hand breaking free from this Polish Diaspora, on the other it was within me. While most London teenagers were getting their first glimpse of up and coming bands like the Beatles, I was listening to operas, symphonies and classical music of all sorts.

The closest I came to a contemporary singer was Edith Piaf, whose voice continues to touch me, to this day. Music, along with my beloved books, formed an ever faithful refuge. The great classical composers could move me to tears, then laughter, followed by tears again. Fun mop top teen tunes seemed more suited to those unencumbered by the burdens I had been born to bear.

Zygmunt demanded that, immediately upon graduation, I go to work to help support the family. I pleaded with him to allow me to go to University. I had worked extraordinarily hard and compiled top grades my last few years at Sacred Heart. Even during the years when I barely slept, I had been able to cram for exams and get good grades. My test scores qualified me for the top schools in the country; I wanted to apply to the prestigious University of London. My father forbade me from even thinking of going away to school. My place was there in the house helping bring money in, until I could find a man stupid enough to marry me.

Dutifully, I went to work and discovered something: I was good at my job. Though a top University was not a possibility, I enrolled in night school where I studied art and history. Shortly thereafter I embarked upon a three month crash course in the secretarial skills I saw as stepping stones into the world of business.

The travails of my home life had broken me down but they had also built into me an intense desire to succeed in life. I treated every day at work, and every night in class, as another step along the path that would one day lead to my escape to a life of independence and freedom. Meanwhile, I was pursuing happiness where I could find it: which was with my friends.

When I was 18, I snuck out to a party one night. I danced with a young man that I had always found attractive. After the party ended, we went out for a walk. We talked as we walked and the night flew by. We ended up at my doorway just as the sun was coming up. He leaned over and I raised my face to him and we kissed. At that moment my father, on his way to morning mass, opened the door.

Zygmunt took one look at what was going on, drew back his fist, and hit me as hard as he could. I literally saw stars as I staggered inside and the horrified boy ran away. Zygmunt didn't bother to say a word, or to check on me, he just continued on to church. I tasted the blood in my mouth and could not imagine how anyone could be so cruel. I had to get away.

In the world I was brought up in, there were only three ways a girl could leave her home: by getting married; by becoming a nun or by being buried in a coffin. I chose marriage.

21

THE ESCAPE
(1962)

When I was 19 a quiet, unassuming young man named Wlodzimierz Olgierd Angus Sreniawa-Borzyslawski (Wlodek) fell in love with me. For the first time, Zygmunt found a young man acceptable. He came from a Polish family and would be a solid provider. I was now nothing but a burden to Zygmunt and he was anxious to clear me out of the house.

Zygmunt pushed me as hard as he could to say, "yes" to Wlodek's ongoing proposals. Wlodek was suddenly invited to every family event. Everywhere I turned; there he was, professing his love for me. There was one problem, I had no romantic feelings for Wlodek; zero.

For an entire year he pursued me but I refused to marry him, hoping for a better option. There was one handsome young man in particular whom I got my knickers in a twist over, but he got another girl pregnant, making his proposal null and void. Finally, realizing there was only one way out of my parent's home, and thinking that perhaps my father was right about no one else ever wanting anything to do with me, I accepted Wlodek's proposal.

I can't remember how Wlodek reacted when I finally said 'yes'. I know that I sighed inside.

22

NO NO NUPTIALS
(1964)

Wlodek was a timid man. In fact he was too timid. Our wedding night was nothing like I thought it would be. Even though I had no desire to sleep with Wlodek, I was a young woman and I was ready to give myself to a man. With this thought in mind, I closed the door of our honeymoon room and glanced over at my new husband with a look that most men would have reacted to with passion.

Whether Wlodek was gay or just completely asexual, I never knew, but that night and every night thereafter, he opted not to consummate our wedding. Since my main reason for getting married was to escape my father's clutches, the sex, or lack thereof, was surprising but in many ways appreciated; for a while.

One immediate benefit of my marriage was that I finally got a passport. My new husband, though of Polish parents, had been born in Scotland and therefore, by extension, I was officially British. Of course, the greatest benefit of my marriage was that I was finally away from my father. For the first time, I slept in a bed in which I knew I was safe, even if a bit bored.

I poured my passion into my work, and I excelled. After a few months of trying odd jobs, a real estate company hired me. This was significant in two ways: it began my lifelong affair with business; especially real estate; and it began my lifelong affair with men. I was not going to be like my mother and endure a loveless marriage. Though I wasn't ready for the drama or derision that a divorce would bring, I was ready for romance. I soon found it.

The company that hired me was a commercial real estate company. Their business was thriving and I loved the challenges that were being thrown my way. I started as a secretary and was running the personnel department within the year. Finally, I was part of something that was positive and rewarding. As part of our business protocol we entertained clients on a regular basis and I was soon considered an indispensable part of the nighttime team.

We would top off the day's work with hours in clubs and pubs, wining and dining our clients. We often went to the very hotspots Nur had taken me to as a wide-eyed teenager. I felt like I was back home when I'd walk into places such as Annabel's, the hottest club in London then; and later, when Princess Diana made it one of her favorite haunts.

After a childhood spent in the shadows, I loved being able to shine. My paychecks bought me a wardrobe that accented my natural assets. I was now, not only aware of how my appearance could affect others, I was taking advantage of it. I enjoyed being in the company of high-powered men. I knew for certain by now that my marriage would never be consummated, and after being robbed of a childhood, I was not going to be robbed of a sex life. My days as a martyr were over.

My boss was a confident man, named David, who was twelve years older than I was; an age difference that was to become a bit of a pattern with me. His cultured ways and relative affluence were appealing. My passions became ignited when he'd come into my office. One night, we were working late and our eyes connected. The question he had been asking me for months was finally answered in the affirmative.

David swept me into his arms and all the passion I had been blocking swept me away to a place of utter ecstasy. Sensations I had never dreamt of coursed through my body as we writhed together on the floor. My eyes lost their ability to focus and I was spirited away. I grasped at his back and I am sure I left my mark on his body. I have no idea how long our first encounter lasted but it felt like an eternity.

Once the genie was out of the bottle, there would be no putting her back. My life was changed and my view of the world would never be the same. The physical passion that had been locked away in a dungeon by nuns, my father and an impotent husband, was set free, and so was I. I could love and I could live.

England in the 'sixties was still the domain of the male chauvinist, but I knew I could compete within it. My hands were firmly on the wheel of my own destiny and I put my foot on the gas. During this time, I decided it was time to do something I'd always wanted to. I was going to drive to Poland.

23

MY HOMELAND
(1965)

I had three weeks worth of vacation saved up and I started making my plans. At first, I was ready to head off on my own to Poland, but even I could see that it would be a foolish thing to do. Wlodek said he'd go with me and in August, of 1965, we set out for the Iron Curtain.

Aside from a couple of quick inexpensive trips down to Spain, this would be our sole vacation together. We were both excited about going. Like me, Wlodek grew up listening to stories about the war and about Poland prior to the invasion. We were both drawn to our parent's homeland like steel to a magnet.

We took the ferry across the Channel and began driving, eventually crossing into Soviet controlled territory via Czechoslovakia. The moment we were through customs, the difference in living conditions was apparent. A few old western cars mingled with the cheap smoking Russian autos that rumbled through the gray streets.

Banners proclaiming the communist cause hung from poles and buildings. There were uniformed men with guns visible throughout the towns. We walked into stores and were stunned by the scarce amount of goods on the empty shelves. The food that was available was of a much lower quality and quantity than anything I was used to seeing. The people we met were always excited to meet someone from 'the West', but at the same time they were subdued. It was as if a cloud hung over their entire existence.

From Czechoslovakia we crossed into Poland. My heart raced as we drove into the land I'd been raised to revere. The same gray world existed in Poland with one definable difference: the Poles had retained their sense of humor. It was as if the country used jokes and laughter, in place of guns and bullets, as a way of showing the Russians that they could never truly defeat them. At one point we went to the home of one of my mother's two surviving sisters, who had stood in line from five o'clock that morning in order to purchase a small amount of ground beef. She was so proud that she was able to serve us such a rare delicacy.

There was a spirit in all the Polish people I met, that made me proud to be connected to them. They were adamant that I let people back home know that the Poles were not communists. They all seemed to hate the ruling regime that used the Soviet military might to club them into sullen submission. The pockmarked walls of their cities served as constant reminders of the evil will their invaders had brought with them. We passed by empty Nazi concentration camps, but I could not bring myself to turn in.

Being in the land of my parents and forefathers helped ground me. After this visit, a piece that had been missing was found.

Like all Poles before me, I too had breathed the air and walked the trails of the land first ruled by King Mieszko in the 11th century.

Driving through Krakow, we could still see the beauty of the city, lying beneath the cold veneer of communism. Warsaw, however, was absolutely devastated. The buildings, which had been there prior to the war, had either been bombed into oblivion or knocked down by tanks. The entire city had been reduced to rubble. In its wake, the Russians had forced the Poles to erect block after block of grey buildings that were bereft of any style or cheer.

Subsequent to my visit there, much of Warsaw would be rebuilt. With most of the records destroyed, the architects had to find references wherever they could. The old town, for example, was rebuilt according to the paintings of the Italian master, Canaletto.

I shared stories with people that had been raised on the same legends as me. I submerged myself in my heritage until I reemerged a more complete version of myself. When it was time for us to drive on, I took a last great gulp of air and felt blessed for having been there. I knew that I would never live in Poland but it would forever be the home of my heritage.

We headed back, crossing into East Germany where the stress level shot up dramatically. As we neared the western border the security tightened. We stopped for a picnic, in a pasture, and watched as a soldier on a motorcycle passed us numerous times.

When we arrived at the border, the motorcycle patrolman was there, along with a row of soldiers, all holding guns. We were pulled off the road and out of our car. I knew that free land was but a short distance away, but I was standing behind the Iron Curtain with a gun pointed at my chest. I soon realized they thought we were trying to smuggle someone out of the country. Our car was almost dismantled, but finally, we were able to recover our passports and cross into West Germany.

The moment we crossed the border, our spirits soared. Bars were bubbling, music was blaring, traffic was rolling and the shelves were stocked with more than scrawny potatoes and vodka. It felt wonderful to be back in the 'free world'. A couple of days later we rolled into London. I was anxious to get back to work in our wonderfully productive capitalistic economy.

24

CARRYING ON
(1966)

Back in England, I dove into my work and into my burgeoning social life. While my husband knowingly looked the other way, I came to know the physical ecstasy that a man and woman can arouse in each other. Though my Catholic mores made shouts of protest, my physical body drowned them out in waves of joy. As stimulating as the sex with David was, the conversations that followed were lacking. I was ready for a new partner in passion.

Wlodek and I had combined our incomes and bought a home, prior to going to Poland. Over time our place became the party house. Wlodek seemed to enjoy having my friends around. Bridge was quite popular, at the time, and Wlodek was a whiz. We would play for hours. Sometimes people would come on a Friday and not leave until Sunday night.

Back in the office, I began a torrid affair with a sharp young executive. His name was Peter Diamond and for the first time in my life I really got my knickers in a twist over someone. Though I was married to Wlodek and having an affair with David, I found myself captivated by Peter's good looks and marvelous personality. Where David was controlling and jealous, Peter was free and outgoing.

David suspected I was involved with another man, but he had no proof. He went so far as to put me into an office kitty-corner to his, so he could see right into it. If another man lingered at my desk, David would instantly be at my door, with some excuse for interrupting.

I was growing bored with David. He would insist that I stay with him late into the evenings, until he'd race off to catch the last train home. He'd call me on the weekends and demand I meet him at a hotel at a moment's notice. Though it had been fun in the beginning, I was tired of his antics. I just needed a final reason, to make me end things with him.

That reason arrived in the guise of his wife who walked into our office one day. One look and I realized I wanted no more to do with this or any married man. I could feel the pain she would feel if she knew what her husband and I were up to. I wasn't naive enough to think I was the first woman he had cheated on his wife with, but I knew his time with me was over.

When I told him we were through, David was crushed. He sat at his desk with a confused look on his face. He fired me on the spot and demanded that I leave, even though I was doing the work of two people. He paid me and told me to never come back. I knew he felt hurt and humiliated, but I could not imagine how he thought our relationship could end any other way.

I was happy to move on. I reveled at the opportunity to find a new and better job. Whoever hired me next would be lucky to do so. I would have no problem finding my next employer. But before I did so, I took two weeks off and flew alone to the Canary Islands.

25

BEAR YOUR OWN CROSS
(1969)

When I boarded the plane, I was a bit drowsy. After saying "hello" to the elderly couple sitting next to me, I nodded off. When I woke up, a handsome man was sitting in their place. He was a pilot, with the airline, and he was going to the islands for his own vacation. During the course of our conversation, I told him where I was staying. We said goodbye, and as I took my taxi into town, I kept thinking about him.

After I had checked in, I went down to swim and when I stepped off the elevator, he was standing right there. I smiled, he held out his arm and we were together for the rest of the time. I experienced love on a tropical beach and our vacation romance was beautiful. Perhaps it could have continued, but he had wounds that rivaled mine. I just wasn't ready or willing to deal with the emotional consequences of his pain.

It turns out, that he had been married to a very beautiful woman who was, in fact, a finalist in the Miss World pageant. About a year before our meeting, she had been killed in a car accident.

He had been driving, but escaped without a scratch. Perhaps, if I did not have my own dark past to come to terms with, I could have seen a life with him, but instead I said goodbye. Once I returned from the islands, I knew it was time to make the move I'd been putting off. It was time to leave my marriage.

One night, soon thereafter, I took Wlodek by the hand, and I told him that it was time for me to move on. I would give him everything, including the house. I truly did feel guilty leaving this gentle yet unfulfilling man. Even though my lawyers would later tell me I was being foolish to give him all of our common property, I refused to take even a penny. Wlodek begged me to stay. He was fine with my dalliances, so long as I would come home to him after each one. He reminded me that if I divorced him, my parents would feel humiliated and my father would be horribly angry.

Though I knew what he said was true, I told Wlodek that it was over. As I knew he would, my husband ran to my parent's home. I packed my things, praying that I would be spared what I knew was coming, but within a few minutes I heard Wlodek's car return.

A moment later, my father burst into our house with fire in his eyes. Wlodek trailed in after him, standing to the side as my father roared at me. I stared at Zygmunt and, while the horrified little girl in me wanted to run away, I stood my ground. Zygmunt spoke to me as if I was a fool to think I had any say in the matter. The more he spoke, the more my spine stiffened.

Zygmunt decreed that I had but three choices: get an annulment; and live at home doing charitable work; or become a nun; or stay in the marriage and bear my cross. I returned his icy stare, as all the rage bubbled up inside me. With a clear voice I told him what I thought about his choices: "You can bear my fucking cross. I'm leaving".

My father was stunned, utterly speechless. He could not comprehend that I had defied him in such a way. In fact, from that moment on, he would never again criticize me to my face, though he would do it ad nausea through my mother. It was as if, once I'd called his bluff, he was afraid of me. As he stood there stupefied, I pushed past the two of them, grabbed a couple of last items and headed out the door.

As I walked away from our house, I knew I was walking away from more than the men behind me. I was turning my back on the entire Polish community that I had been raised within. While there was a sensation of fear, I felt the sun shining down and for the first time in my life I felt free. A refugee no longer, I knew in that moment that this life was mine, and I was the one in charge of it. The fear that had kept me imprisoned for so long, no longer had any hold on me. Basia was born anew.

26

MOVING ON UP

As I reached for the door of my vintage, why say "old" when "vintage" sounds so much better, mini-cooper, I threw my hair back into the air, sat behind the controls and drove off into a new life. I was breathing deep, feeling the oxygen pump through my pulsating body. Every nerve was on fire. Awakened to the joys of physical passion, I now added the elixir of personal power and independence to the mix.

My fears and phobias had all flickered away with the blinks of my dumbfounded father's unseeing eyes. I would not speak to the man nor see him for a whole year. When we would again meet, he would no longer hold me captive with his withering words. His ability to control my young emotions was gone. He held no sway over my life any longer. I shook my head in wonder and let out a yelp of glee. I now decided where I would go, whom I would see, what I would do and when I would do it.

Ironically, Wlodek would actually move into my parent's home for a year, praying with my mother each night, in hope that God would return me to him. I felt sorry for Wlodek. I knew his world seemed to be coming to an end. However, in that moment, I focused on my world, which was just beginning to open up.

I rolled through the streets of London and they suddenly looked more modern, as if the old Victorian Polish culture of my parents had somehow shrouded the city in cold stone and foreboding buildings. This was suddenly, the London of 1969, which was alive and reverberating with sounds, colors and opportunity.

Since I was already a pariah in my parent's eyes, I decided to compound things. I drove to the house of a man named Victor, with whom I had recently become involved. He shared the home with a couple of other young people. He invited me in and I ended up living with him for the next year.

Victor was a gorgeous man, but more of a delightful diversion than a serious suitor. He was a very successful tour manager, whose business took him away for weeks at a time, which was perfect. Now, that I was free of my past, I was ready to work for my future. I knew that it was time to find a company that I could go somewhere with.

When I had interviewed before, I had gone in as a demure young lady who hoped she could find a nice position with a nice company. Now, I was walking into interviews with an aura of confidence and a bearing that was intimidating to some and irresistible to others. I was looking for a career path.

One of my first appointments brought me to the office of Andrew McLaglen, and he found me irresistible. Andrew had just directed a movie called "Shenandoah" which was a huge hit, starring James Stewart. The tagline of the movie was "It shakes the screen like cannon thunder" and that is how Andrew came on to me; like cannon thunder.

Our meeting took place in Andrew's private apartment, in one of the most prestigious areas of London. In the course of our meeting he told me that while he'd love to have me as his assistant, he'd prefer me as his lover and global travel companion. I turned the assistant job down, but had a short-lived but very passionate affair with Andrew. This was my first taste of the glamorous world of movies and I enjoyed it.

I found that many of the men I interviewed with over the next week or two seemed to have the same intentions when it came to spending time with me. England was a chauvinistic enclave, which viewed women as something to view. Finally, I walked through the doors of a company that would be a place of transformation for me.

27

ALFA-LAVAL

Alfa-Laval had been created by Gustav de Laval, inventor of the centrifuge. Alfa-Laval, was owned by a multi-national conglomerate based in Sweden. The company did everything from manufacturing and selling farm equipment, to building massive heat exchangers and centrifuges for production plants. I interviewed for a position in the marketing department and I got it.

On my first day of work, I reported to the assigned office and sat down waiting for my new boss. I waited and I waited and I waited. Finally, a finely dressed man wandered in. His name was Ron Fennel and he would be my immediate supervisor.

Ron was responsible for every major event the company threw, as well as every brochure and press release. He was an eccentric man who had a natural knack for coming up with great ideas. The details, however, were of no interest to Ron and his previous assistant had been unable to cope with his lack of focus. Luckily for me, and Ron, details were something I was a master of.

When the big things in life are too devastating to deal with, one learns to love the little things that one can actually control.

In order to insure nothing fell through the cracks, I started my day at Ron's desk and didn't move until I'd wrestled the last bit of information out of him. In short order, I took control of every project on the docket. Ron was immediately impressed and only too happy to pass on more and more of the work that crossed his desk. He soon started sending me out, in his place, for presentations and meetings to some of our more remote offices. Ron was a big city boy, period.

I became a regular at Ron's daily lunches and dinners at the top hotels and restaurants in London. Ron's expense account was virtually bottomless and he did his best to prove it. I found myself back at the Savoy Hotel and amongst many of my old favorite haunts.

If I wasn't sipping champagne, the most likely place to find me was at the office. Late at night, I'd be prowling the mimeograph department, flashlight in hand, making copies for a morning meeting. It didn't matter what was asked of me, I did it, and much more.

One of the secretaries asked me why I was working so hard. She pointed out that of the 5,000 people that worked for Alfa-Laval, not one of them was a female executive. Everyone knew, there was a glass ceiling that stopped women from advancing.

It didn't matter how hard I worked, she said, I'd never get anywhere. I looked at her and smiled. I didn't bother to explain myself. Somehow I knew I was going to be the woman that changed things: I would smash through the glass ceiling no matter what it took.

28

THE BIG BREAK
(1970)

While Ron was undeniably fun to work with, he was also an extraordinary challenge. Ron had no problem going on vacation, right before a conference, leaving me alone to handle everything. The man was either supremely confident in my skills or completely irresponsible. In either case, I was consistently able to pull things together and make us both look good to the man he reported to: Brian Kent.

Brian had become president of the company just shortly before my arrival, and he was intensely focused on raising the productivity of the company. Brian was a big believer in corporate communication and live sales events. As a result of this, Ron and I were responsible for an endless array of luncheons, conferences, retreats, sales events, symposiums and branding initiatives.

Brian was very hands on and insistent that our events come off without a hitch. One way or another they normally did. One day Ron came in with news that we were putting together the most important conference that the company had ever had. The entire board of directors was flying in, from Sweden, for a series of meetings, set at offices around the country, at which Brian was going to systematically unveil his new 5-year plan for Alfa-Laval.

Brian was insistent that everything had to be perfect. Nothing could go wrong. The successful presentation of his master plan was essential. His very presidency was riding on the outcome of this complex conference. No expense was to be spared.

Well, those were the words Ron loved to hear, and we immediately went off to the Savoy hotel for a caviar and champagne-laced brainstorming session. By the time we were through, we'd put together an itinerary that started with a private train ride from London to Cardiff and then continued on to other cities where the board of directors would visit our various regional offices.

We had entertainment to book, helicopters to schedule, speakers to alert, brochures to print, trains to rent, flights to book, transport vehicles to mobilize and meals to cater. Before we could get any of these things done, Ron disappeared on one of his incessant holidays. One week passed, then two, and finally another. Although I was keeping things going, there were a number of decisions that had to be made or we would be jeopardizing the mission.

Finally, I went to Brian's secretary and asked for a meeting. Brian called me in and I told him exactly where we were at: NOWHERE. He immediately saw that we couldn't wait any longer for Ron's return. I assured him that I was ready to step in and take over all aspects of the preparation, I just needed his authorization. He gave me a quick glance, as he thought through his options, and then told me to proceed. He wanted daily reports and immediate notice of any problems I could not handle.

I walked out of Brian's office and hit the ground running. I was firing up the printing department at night, putting presentations together on weekends and signing contracts over breakfast. The other people in the department were useless. It was clear to me that they would rather see me fail, especially the men. Their attitudes only made me work harder.

Ron returned in time to make sure everyone knew he was back. In the meantime, I was the one going through the final checklists with Brian and assuring him that we had everything covered. Though I had done the work, I was happy to have Ron back. His quirky personality always brightened my mood.

From the moment the first flights started arriving, things moved like clockwork. No sooner would an executive step foot outside the airport, they would have a person taking their bags and driving them to their next stop. Brochures and programs were given to each executive as they checked in. Every detail was taken care of, down to the seating charts Brian and I had put together for each meal, session and train ride. The conference was a smashing success. The board of directors gave their stamp of approval and the company's executives were excited about the new areas of growth that meant bonuses and raises.

Back in London, Brian casually walked into my office one afternoon. He told me that he was thrilled with how things turned out and my performance. He cut right to the purpose of his visit and offered me a choice of two promotions. The first would make me one of the top assistants in the company with far more duties and a raise. The second would make me the first female executive in the company.

I held my breath for a moment as his words registered in my mind. There was no choice to make, immediately I told him that I'd like to be an executive. Brian smiled and held out his hand. I shook it, as I looked him in the eye. I think we could both feel the glass ceiling cracking.

29

CRASH GOES THE GLASS

The person who headed internal operations for Brian was retiring. I was suddenly in charge of everything from the procurement of desks, to oversight of the 200-strong fleet of company cars, to the state of the company's employee cafeterias. I hired the women who answered the phones, the men that ran the printing department, and the company who cleaned the building. When Brian had walked into my office I was an assistant in the PR department, when he walked out I was overseeing the day-to-day duties of over 50 people.

As soon as Brian left, less enlightened men were already plotting my demise. It seems that while they found me nice to look at and seemingly good at my job, the concept of taking orders from a woman was something that they were unwilling to do. The proud male executives of Alfa-Laval were not taking kindly to the thought of a woman joining their ranks. Male chauvinism was alive and well in England, in the late 'sixties. As one of the first women, in London, to challenge the corporate status quo, I was an anomaly and I was a target.

I would walk into restrooms and hear women speaking about me, only to see them turn red, when I'd walk up next to them. More than one man quit, unable to adapt to a world where a woman could have authority over them. Other men tried to sabotage me with nefarious memos and unsigned letters railing about my failings.

Men would make cracks about me wearing too much make-up and women would make cracks about me not wearing enough. Many secretaries, instead of celebrating the fact that the youngest executive in the company was now a woman, would wonder aloud, "how long had I'd been sleeping with Brian?"

While I ignored petty gossip, I gave no quarter when it came to being treated professionally. One day, I was walking down the hall, when one of the company's directors, who held rank over me, yelled out to me. Instead of calling me by my first name, or Mrs. Bory (the shortened version of my last name that I went by at that time), he rudely yelled out "Bory." I could feel everyone turning to see how I'd react. Instead of walking over to him, I turned my head, gave him a scathing look, turned on my heels and walked away, without a word. About an hour later, he came into my office and apologized.

The suspicions about Brian and me could not have been further from the truth. Brian Kent had always been, and would always be, a complete gentleman. Brian was happily married and focused on two things: his family and Alfa-Laval. He had a brilliant business mind and saw in me, someone he could mold.

I had already learned a great amount from Brian. Watching him create a five-year plan and sell it to the board, had been a tremendous experience. Brian drilled into me the need to execute and produce. Things had to get done and they had to get done right. One by one, I put his business tenets into my mental filing system, ready to be drawn upon, whenever needed.

I loved my new position and I threw myself into it with total abandon. My enthusiasm was such that it could not be doused, even when I discovered, that I was only making half what the male executives were making. On top of that I was the only executive in the company not getting one of the two hundred company cars that I was in charge of.

The truth was that I couldn't get more than miffed at the slight. The opportunity was too great to waste energy on sour grapes. Besides, even at half of one of my male peer's salary, the job came with a raise. Plus, I had a secretary and an assistant all to myself.

In reality, many of the men and women I worked with were quite professional. It became easy for me to ignore the others. After growing up under the accusatory eyes of the nuns and old Polish refugee women, a few memos, whispers and glances were nothing. I wasn't intimidated one bit. I charged forward and made the most of my opportunity. I knew that if I did my job, everything else would take care of itself.

The person who had held the position before me had retired due to an illness that had affected his performance. As a result, when I took over, the department was in a shambles. I set it as my goal to finally get things running as smooth as possible.

I finally was able to forego my flashlight, as I found out how to turn the lights on, after hours. I spent every available moment insuring that my department over-performed. I renegotiated the service agreement on our cars; I modernized our office machines and improved the overall effectiveness of everyone in my department. On top of my new duties, I continued to get called upon to pull Ron's arse out of the fire. I was working around the clock and I loved it.

The first thing I realized was that there was no organization, in my department. As a product of a Catholic schooling, I knew how to schedule and organize things. I interviewed everyone that worked for me. I then put each of the five sharpest people in charge of nine others. Overnight, things changed.

Brian had his eccentric in Ron, and he had his office operations person in me. He had more key people in finance, sales and manufacturing. Alfa-Laval was humming along and growing at a fast clip. Brian's five-year plan was off to a great start.

Every now and then, I would think about the disparity in pay. On top of my new duties, Ron was still coming to me for help on every conference and out of town symposium. It didn't make me depressed, but it did get me thinking that I'd love the chance, one day, to work for myself and set my own wages. The itch that I would go on to scratch, for most of the rest of my life, had started.

30

BON VOYAGE VICTOR
(1971)

During this time, my mother's endless quiet prayers hit their mark and I agreed to come home for the traditional Polish Christmas Eve dinner. I was bound by longstanding tradition; I could not just abandon my parents. No matter their faults, I would not allow myself to be considered an ingrate and have them humiliated in the eyes of their peers. Victor and I arrived at my parent's door, almost a year after I had walked out on Wlodek. During that time my mother had come to meet me at coffee shops, but there had been no communication between Zygmunt and me.

It is incredible the lengths we go to, in order to keep the facade of family together. Seeing my father, only dredged up memories that I would rather forget. Thinly veiled criticisms still flowed from Zygmunt's mouth, but they no longer hurt me. The man had lost his power.

A few weeks later, Victor called me from Italy and told me he had good news. He was on his way home for a four-month stay.

Our happy home life had been built on a foundation of personal space. His new work schedule was about to change everything. I decided that if Victor was going to be there more, I was out the door.

Before Victor was back, I moved out of the flat he'd bought a few months earlier. I picked him up at the airport and broke it to him as gently as I could. He took it badly. I had never considered Victor as a potential husband, so it greatly surprised me when he handed me a beautiful handbag that had my first name embroidered in front of his last name.

I looked Victor in the eye, and told him I was sorry but what we had was over. Victor was angry and sad. His sense of male machismo had been wounded and he said things that I'm sure he later regretted. After he'd finished with his rampage, I wished him well and headed to my new home.

I had moved into a sharp apartment in an attractive part of the city. When my brother turned 18, he moved in with me, desperate to escape the cold clutches of Zygmunt. Though he had not suffered physically, as I had, he had not been spared from our father's vindictive nature. Remarkably, Richard had emerged as a charismatic, young man, intent on becoming an actor.

Richard was basically a kid who knew little of the ways of the world. When it came to rent, for example, he thought he was only supposed to pay for the actual time he spent in the apartment. When he'd be off shooting a TV show or a movie, he'd deduct that time from his bill. It was more amusing than annoying.

Richard really was a good actor, who would go on to appear in a number of top films, including "The Eagle Has Landed", which was a hugely successful movie. There was a quaint joy I got out of living with my baby brother for this short slice of time.

On the romantic front, I was not involved with anyone on a serious level, though there were men around. Tall, physical Victor made a few return appearances, but nothing more than a night here and there. I was constantly interacting with strong businessmen who were natural leaders and in command of large personal or business accounts. Some of these men became temporary lovers, though none got my knickers in a twist.

These were heady and fulfilling times at work. One day I found myself being asked by Ron to step in and help him put on a symposium. The particular project Ron needed help on was to take place at a hotel that had been booked, but not properly prepped. A hundred or so executives were about to arrive for a symposium that wasn't close to being ready.

There would be two other men, not associated with the symposium, arriving at the hotel as well. They would become two of the most important people I would ever meet. One would ultimately be very good for me and the other would be very bad.

31

THE WRONG DON

Ron had gone off again, only to return to find himself in a fix. There were a thousand details left to be taken care of and he came to me; desperate for my assistance. I knew the drill and went to work insuring that everything would be fine. As usual Brian was quite involved and extremely demanding. Perfection was the goal in every operation we ran.

I arrived at the Skyline Hotel, the weekend before people would start showing up. I had reserved every part of the hotel I could, including the entire pool area, which occupied the center of the hotel's lobby and was surrounded by coffee shops and an atrium. If you weren't a guest of Alfa-Laval, you weren't using the pool for a few days. We were unveiling our newest heat exchangers, which sold for a pretty penny. We were going to make sure our buyers had every reason to spend their pennies with us. We spared no expense in making sure the symposium was a success.

To give you an idea of how involved Brian was, and how committed I was: I spent a night repainting the floor upon which our sales models would be standing, because Brian thought the floor clashed with the colors of our machines. The hotel had no one on hand that could do it, and everyone else had gone, so I got on my knees and painted through the night.

The same day I arrived, two men named Don, checked into the Skyline Hotel. They had both flown in from America, on business. They were both extremely successful and precisely twelve years older than me. They would both have profound effects upon my life. One of them would affect me in a very positive way. This Don's last name was Fuller, and this was not the first time we had been in the same place.

Nearly thirty years earlier, British mid-shipman Donald Fuller had stood on the deck of the ship that guarded my departure from Palestine. Don was a wide-eyed lad of sixteen that day, having joined the prestigious Dartmouth, Naval Academy the year before. He had gone on to serve six years in the Royal British Navy, during which time; he competed in the 1952 Olympics as a member of the British water polo team. He left the Navy to complete his education, which culminated with a Masters Degree in physics from Cambridge.

Subsequently, Don had gone to America where he had made his fortune. He was back in England on a business trip, in his role as CEO of Microdata, one of the more successful computer companies in the United States. After settling in and spending his first couple days there preparing for meetings, he decided to take a swim on Monday morning; the first day of the symposium.

To his great consternation, Don was told that the pool was closed for a private event. Flummoxed, Don asked to speak to the person running the event. But he did not get to speak to that person, for I was unavailable and in the midst of a breakfast with the other Don.

In retrospect, how I wish I had been able to sit down and discuss the situation with Don Fuller. However, I didn't. As fate would have it, after he had checked in, this other Don, Don Wheeler, came down to a café where I happened to be sitting, reviewing my notes. I looked up, in search of a waitress. It was then that I noticed this striking man sitting nearby, waiting to place his order as well. We realized, at the same time, that the café we were in wasn't open yet.

I packed up my things and went one way and he went the other. When I reached the door to the nearest alternative, he was standing there. He introduced himself as Don Wheeler and invited me to join him for breakfast. I agreed and sat down at a table with him. It was at this point that I began to speak to Don Wheeler, my future husband, business partner extraordinaire, and finally, my attempted assassin.

Oh yes, that morning, I spoke to the wrong Don.

32

WHEELER THE WONDER
(1972)

Don Wheeler was handsome, wickedly smart and used to traveling the world in utter style, although it impressed him little. Don was an engineering genius, who had no trouble telling those he worked with that they were not. The night I met him, he was on his way to meet with the giant Russian purchasing agency, Machinoimport. To that point in history, no American had ever made a deal with Machinoimport. Don Wheeler was about to be the first.

He instantly struck me as unique, with his bolo tie, brilliant intellect and a personality that combined the American can-do spirit with brash confidence. In the beginning he greatly underplayed his business success. I had no idea that he commanded a multi-million dollar company that was about to grow much larger. He never spoke of the company in terms of it being all his. Nor did he mention the thousand of acres of oil land he owned in Pennsylvania. I found these things out much later.

Immediately, Don and I had chemistry. We began spending a great deal of time together as his business brought him back to England on an ongoing basis. There was no doubt about it: I was getting my knickers in a twist over this American. Within the year, Don opened a plant outside London and we found ourselves falling in love.

Don had been one of US Steel's top engineers, but he had no patience for company politics. When he was asked his opinion, he gave it with no thought as to who his words might offend. There was no way around it, Don was an impossible employee and was eventually fired. Outraged, he went home and sealed himself in his empty garage.

He spent the next three months building a steel welding machine that he believed would transform the industry. Large trucks would pull up to his home with deliveries of all sorts. He made countless trips to hardware stores and slept but a few hours a day. The end result was a machine that welded steel more efficiently and economically than was ever before possible.

Don's first sale was to US Steel, the very company that had fired him. In order to make the delivery, Don had to take the garage door off. He received his first check and his company, Guild International, was born. Since then he'd been busy booking business all over the world.

I didn't know any of this for months. In the beginning there was nothing in Wheeler's bearing or demeanor that led me to think he was rich. I did think he was smart, sharp, confident, good looking, strong and opinionated.

To understand the force that Don was, what happened when he left the Skyline hotel the day we met and flew on to Russia, is quite illustrative. When Don landed in Russia, he was met at the airport by a gray suited man with a trench coat. They drove in silence to a Moscow hotel where Wheeler was checked in and "assigned" to a room. He was told to wait there and he would be contacted when he was needed.

For four days, Wheeler sat in his room and twiddled his thumbs. Finally, there was a call and he was told that a cab, with a specific license plate number, would be waiting for him downstairs, in the morning. He awoke the next day and was driven to a converted palace. Once inside, he was shuffled into an opulent meeting room, where twelve serious-looking men sat on one side of a long table. Don was given the lone chair on the other side.

The Machinoimport bureaucrats proceeded to drone on and on, via a translator, about the glories of the Russian Empire and the capitalist failings of the west. Don listened as long as his patience allowed, which was not more than a few minutes, and then he held up his hand, for silence. He closed his notebook and said: "Gentlemen, when you are ready to do business, call me at the hotel". He stood up and walked out of the room, signaled his driver and returned to his hotel. He waited for four more days, before getting the call he was betting they'd make.

Wheeler was driven back and seated in the same meeting room. This time, the discussion was about his new machines and how they worked. He walked out with a seven million dollar contract in his hand.

I was long fascinated by entrepreneurs and especially those I'd met from America. There was an American optimism and spirit that I found intoxicating. When I was young, my parents had applied to immigrate to America, but were told that my sister would not be allowed to accompany them due to her affliction. My mother refused to even dream of such a scenario, of leaving her behind, and so we stayed in England. Still, from that point on, I had dreamt of going to America.

As my relationship with Wheeler grew, so to did my desire to strike out on my own. For the first time, I began thinking about leaving Alfa-Laval.

33

LEAVING LONDON
(1973)

I met Don Wheeler in May, 1972, and for the first six months, we eased our way into a relationship that grew stronger, more physical and more passionate with each meeting. When I was not working, I was meeting Don somewhere for a tryst. We spent our weekends in the most beautiful hotels of cities such as Paris, Athens, Dubrovnik and Copenhagen. We fell in love and began talking about a future together. I had not been looking to get married again, but suddenly I was heading directly in that direction.

In January, 1973, Wheeler asked me to come to America, marry him and be a part of his company. When Don proposed the idea, I realized I'd had my fill of the British corporate world and was ready for a fresh start. This was my chance to go to the world's most vibrant country, with a man I loved. I agreed and we began making plans.

There was some trepidation. In reality, I knew very little about this man. I knew that he was divorced, that he was extremely intelligent and had enough business going, to allow him to stay in top hotels around the world. My worries increased one day when I called Wheeler from England to wish him goodnight in America.

The phone rang and Wheeler answered, but as soon as I said "hello" the phone was handed over to another man, who I happened to know. He was a business associate of Wheeler's, who had been there the first time we'd met. He hemmed and hawed trying to come up with a good reason why Wheeler couldn't speak to me right then.

The next time we spoke, I dragged the truth out of Don. He had been living with a woman when we met, but he swore to me that she was on her way out of his life for good. In fact, he said, I had called in the midst of her being told they were through.

Discovering that Don was living with another woman, while courting me, was unacceptable. I cut things off. Don spent the next weeks winning me back, swearing there was nothing more between them and that I was the only woman that meant anything to him. His charm and the thought of going to America were ultimately too intoxicating a combination. I put Wheeler's indiscretions behind me and told him that I would come to America and marry him.

34

COMING TO AMERICA

It amazed me how far things had progressed in my life. A couple years earlier, I had been excommunicated from my family for daring to leave a facade of a marriage. Now, they were begging me to stay in London. My mother was scared she would never see me again and my father was worried I'd stop sending them monthly support payments. I promised my mother I'd return every year for a visit, and I ignored my father.

Telling Brian that I was leaving was not easy, but I saw an opportunity that was too good to pass up. The next great adventure of my life lay before me and there was nothing that would keep me from jumping at it. Ultimately, Brian understood that this was something I had to do.

I flew to Ohio in May 1973, one year after we had shared our breakfast at the Skyline Hotel. Don met me in Cleveland, at the airport, in his Cadillac. We spent the night in a hotel, where I had lobster tail for the first time but definitely not the last. The next morning, we set out for Pennsylvania towards a "plot" of land he owned along the Allegheny River. Green forests filled my vision as the sun shone down on land that could have come right out of the lyrics of "America the Beautiful."

The "plot" turned out to be one thousand of the most beautiful acres of land I'd ever seen. It was bordered on one side by a mile of the Allegheny River. Wheeler owned two and a half mountains and the valleys between them. When I first arrived, the land was filled with oil rigs and a lone, isolated house, which sat five hundred feet above the river. Views from every room went for miles and were absolutely spectacular.

One of the first things I noticed, about the decor, were the loaded shotguns over every door to the house. I asked Wheeler why and he said that a policeman had told him that if someone was on his property, he could shoot him or her on the spot. Then, all he had to do was drag them into the house and proclaim self-defense. I later learned that he was referred to by the locals as "The Mad Millionaire."

The very first night there, I was about to get into the sunken tub, for a romantic bath, when Wheeler suddenly told me to "freeze." I looked around and he was standing there with one of his guns. I looked to see what he was pointing it at, and as I looked over, he shot and killed a large copperhead snake that was less than five feet away from me.

We continued on with our romantic rites before finally turning out the lights. Before I could fall asleep, I heard a light flapping sound. I turned the light on and there, flying around the room, was a bat. I almost turned to Wheeler to tell him that I was heading back to England. Instead, we shooed the bat out a window and, finally, I fell asleep.

Later, I would go on to deal with more snakes than I care to recall. Including one time, when I'd had to chop the head off of a huge copperhead in order to stop it from killing one of our dogs. I thought of shooting it, but chose a shovel instead, afraid I'd shoot the dog or myself, by mistake.

After my eventful first night, I awoke to find Wheeler ready to get to work. He handed me a hard hat and a few minutes later I was helping him repair the oil wells that had broken during his absence. We would attach rods to cables and extract them from the thousand feet deep wells, fix or replace the broken parts and then send them back down into the abyss below. When we'd finish, I would stand back and watch as the green crude oil slowly started gurgling out into the waiting collector barrels.

I loved our oil. It was green, rich and thick, with a fragrance that I found lovely. When I would get a cut, I would rub some of the oil on it and the cut would heal soon thereafter. Well over a century before, the very first oil well in the world had been sunk just a few miles away, in a town called Titusville. When the barrels were full, a truck would drive in, siphon the oil and drive off to a nearby refinery.

By the time events would force me to leave this beautiful place, five years the in the future, the land would be filled with a new lake, cabins, a restaurant and miles of trails for our visitors. We would call it Buzzard's Point-Silver Valley and it would be one of the premier resorts in Pennsylvania.

I soon learned that Wheeler owned an assortment of companies that included Guild International, Wheeler Oil and Wheeler Real Estate. The day I arrived is the day I took over the books of the latter two companies and all our personal accounts. My life quickly took on a new series of responsibilities. Once a week, I would drive to Ohio, with Wheeler, and review the status of every project in process at Guild International. These trips soon turned into solo excursions, as Wheeler decided his time would be better spent at home in front of the fire, especially during the winter when the roads were covered with snow and black ice.

My first project at Guild International was to jump into the middle of the huge Russian order that Wheeler had received, right after we first met. What I learned was that Wheeler had given the bank a personal guarantee, as they would not loan him the money, based upon the contract. Normally, transactions like this were secured with letters of credit and the Russians had not issued one.

No bank had ever seen a Russian contract before and they weren't about to loan money in the hopes that it would be honored, especially since it was written in Russian. Thus, the loans Wheeler needed to fulfill the order were secured by his land and other business holdings. For the first year of our life together, I helped oversee the construction and ultimate delivery of the giant steel welding machines, which the Russians had ordered.

Besides the assembled machines, they had also ordered ten years worth of spare parts. This became my area of direct responsibility. I was taught how to read the blue prints, pull out the parts numbers and make the orders. To this day, I wonder if the Russians really got all the correct parts they needed, as I was not an engineer.

As the machines came closer to being ready to ship, the tension grew. We were directed to break the machines down, put them into crates and deliver them to a Russian ship that would take them across the ocean. Once the captain verified the content of the crates, we would be wired the money within ten days. At least, that was what the agreement said.

We made our delivery on time to the captain and watched as the massive crates were lowered into the hull of the mighty ship. We returned home and waited nervously for the wire. After ten days, it wasn't there and there was no word from Russia.

After twenty days, we were frantic and our calls and telexes to Moscow were bouncing back from the satellite, unanswered. It looked as if Wheeler's business was going to be destroyed. Without the payments from Russia, he'd lose almost everything. Right when we were convinced we'd been swindled, we received a call from the bank. Seven million dollars had just appeared in our account, without word or warning. We were saved and we had millions of dollars in the bank.

From the time I'd arrived, we'd been planning a large wedding but week-by-week the complexities of flying friends and family in from England was making the whole idea tiresome. We were in Houston for a meeting, when we both decided it would be much easier and more romantic just to elope. That's what we did.

We drove to Neiman-Marcus where I bought a beautiful wedding gown. We flew to Las Vegas and had our cab driver stop off at the court house where we got our marriage license and then take us directly to the Hitching Post Chapel.

We were married in August 1973, by the good Reverend Peter Love. His wife served as our witness and graciously pushed the 'play' button on the portable tape recorder that provided our wedding music. That night we celebrated on the strip and loved like there was no tomorrow.

We cut our honeymoon short when I received a call from my longtime friend Frances, who was in New York with her husband, and my God-Child, Lizzie, hoping to come see me. We met them back in Pennsylvania and I showed them the beautiful forests, mountains and valleys that were now half mine.

Even though I was as busy as could be, with all the work Wheeler had thrown at me, he still wanted me to get a job in town. Though Franklin was a small city, three major corporations had manufacturing plants and offices there. One of these companies was called Chicago Pneumatics.

I went in as a secretary and within a month they asked me to take over their public relations department, emulating much of what I'd done at Alfa-Laval. The moment they offered me this position, Wheeler suddenly decided he needed me, full time. It was at this precise moment that we got the idea to turn our thousand acres of land into a resort and conference center. From that moment on, every spare second of my time was spent helping build the Wheeler business empire, the centerpiece of which would be called Buzzard Point-Silver Valley.

During the week, we lived in near isolation, until I was able to build up a circle of friends in the nearby community. Though Wheeler suggested I trade my designer dresses in for overalls from JC Penny's, I was able to find shops in the prestigious town of Shaker Heights, Ohio, which had the type of fashions I fancied. Wheeler had visions of turning his property into one of the premier resort communities in Pennsylvania and I was one hundred percent on board with him. We drew a master plan and soon set to work.

35

BUILDING BUZZARD'S POINT
(1974)

The centerpiece of our resort was to be a 10-acre lake with a conference facility high above, carved right out of the other side of the mountain, looking out over the Allegheny. In order to create the lake, Wheeler drew up plans for an eighty-foot high earthen dam that was three hundred and twenty foot thick at its base. In the era of Earth Day and the conservationist movement, Wheeler had no time for environmental studies or permits. He made his calculations and we went to work.

Wheeler, a small crew and I put on hardhats and hopped on the bulldozers, crawler-loaders and backhoes that we'd bought. Always looking for an angle, we set up a small side business renting our equipment out during the winter, which added another hundred thousand dollars a year to the bottom line. There is no discounting the fact that Wheeler was a brilliant businessman. Once the payment came in from Russia, we never had to even think about money, other than as to how we were going to invest and spend it.

I took the wheel, literally, with Buzzard's Point. While Don was playing with his bulldozers, I was handling every detail involved with launching a major resort: from the books; to the personnel; to the contracts; if it had anything to do with Buzzard's Point, it went across my desk. Plus, I put my share of time in, behind the wheels of the dozers.

We worked hard during the day and spent our nights going over the plans for the resort we were going to build. Don was Tarzan and I was Jane. Wheeler felt like he was above the law, on his property, and the thought of getting permission to build out his vision didn't cross his mind. Every time I'd bring it up, he'd have a fit and say it was his land and he could do what he wanted on it. It did not help that the newly formed local planning commission was toothless, consisting of an alcoholic lawyer, an ex-grave digger and a doctor's wife.

Besides, Don Wheeler figured he knew better than anyone else how to build a dam. He didn't even bother with plans, we just got to work. Day after day, we dug out the sides of the valley, widening it in the process, and transported millions of pounds of dirt over to the dam. I would drive the bulldozers and back hoes, right along with Don and our small crew.

The first thing we did was drop a giant steel pipe into the river that ran through our valley, on its way to the nearby Allegheny. This allowed us to pile dirt on top of the riverbed, without stopping the flow of the water. Slowly but surely, our dam grew. It was in the middle of winter when we finally finished it. We still needed to put an emergency spillway in, but we decided we'd finish that up in the spring, when the earth was again soft.

A diver went into the river and closed off the pipe so that the water began rising behind the dam. About sixty feet up, a spillway pipe that connected back down to the pipe in the river bed was awaiting the rising water. Once the lake got high enough the water would flow down it and continue its journey to the Allegheny.

Hour by hour our little lake grew. Within a few days we had a beautiful 10-acre lake that stretched back into the valley. The land that rose up from the water would soon hold lovely cabins and vacation homes meant for the enjoyment of people, from as far away as New York City.

The weight generated by a sixty-foot deep lake is immense, yet our homemade dam was holding up just fine, that is, until a massive snowstorm hit. Tons of snow landed on the mountains and then, overnight, a thaw set in. The temperature shot up into the sixties, the sun came out and the snow started melting. We were a little nervous but the pipe seemed to be keeping up with the melting snow and the lake stayed level. Then it started to rain.

The rain poured down and within a few hours the combination of rain and melting snow sent a deluge of water into our valley. Don and I stood on the top of the dam looking down and, as we watched, we could see the water rising. The water flowing out through the spillway was insignificant compared to the amount of water flowing into the lake. If we didn't do something fast, the rising water would breech the dam and the whole thing would give way, sending a deluge down upon unsuspecting riverfront homes.

The only chance we had to avert disaster was to dig our emergency spillway immediately, where the dam joined the mountain. A job that should take a week was going to have to be done in twelve hours, under flood lights, in a pouring deluge. Wheeler and I each jumped on a bulldozer and along with a couple other workers, on backhoes and crawler-loaders, we fought the elements through the night. Water was threatening to dissolve the ground beneath our massive vehicles. I heard a shout and looked over to see Don's dozer about to tumble into the water. He was saved at the last second when one of our workers drove up and pushed his vehicle back onto solid ground. Against all odds, we carved out a channel just as the lake was about to breech the dam, the spillway opened and disaster was averted.

Too exhausted to celebrate, Don and I collapsed into each other's arms and retreated to our bed to sleep for an entire day. After that Wheeler boasted about how well his dam worked, while I could only think about how close we had come to destroying a number of homes with his contraband dam.

36

CRACKS IN THE FOUNDATION

Such adventures filled our days for next three years as our resort grew. During this time, I became the public face of the Buzzard's Point-Silver Valley project. I was quoted in the paper, interviewed for the news, friendly with the mayor, a frequent visitor to chamber of commerce meetings and the one who met with the lawyers. People began to forget about Wheeler, and every once and a while, I could tell that it was starting to bother him. However, for the most part we were both happy and far too busy to worry about the little things.

I was deeply in love with Don and extremely content. I've always been drawn to men with intelligence and character, and no one could deny that Wheeler was a character. He was an obstinate cuss, but he was also ingeniously clever and creative. Our venture was going splendidly, give or take the odd disaster.

I was in charge of the press, operations and promotion, as I had been in London. Wheeler was in charge of finances and providing the grand vision. The partnership and the marriage were both working. I even enjoyed the times, in the winter, when I'd be left alone for a month at a time, while Wheeler went off on a sales junket. I'd watch over our land with our five dogs as my companions, and spend my time reading and listening to classical music.

I flew my parents over, though at separate times. I knew that they were each more enjoyable on their own. When my father arrived, it was the first time I felt he approved of what I was doing. He loved our land. He'd wake up and set off on long hikes, cherishing the natural solitude and beauty of our valleys.

My mother was far less adventurous, but no less impressed with the scale and scope of what we were doing. Wheeler's mother also joined us one time, but her time there was fraught with tension, as she and her son had not spoken since his divorce. In their exchanges I got my first glimpse of a selfish and mean side of Wheeler that I did not like.

There were other signs as well, that were beginning to give me cause for concern. Wheeler's first marriage had produced seven children, yet he seemed to only speak to two of them. His ex-wife was treated as a pariah and I saw him go out of his way to cause her, and the kids, hardship. His support payments almost always went out late and never without a fight. He had cut one of his sons out of his life simply for refusing to get a hair cut. I told him I thought his behavior was appalling, and he told me to mind my own business.

Aside from these skirmishes, our time in Buzzard's Point continued to be enjoyable. When we were just starting the dam we found ourselves playing host to a team of Russian engineers for three months. They had been sent over by the government to learn all they needed to know about the new machines they had ordered.

During the week they would be at the manufacturing plant in Ohio, with a translator, learning the ins and outs of the technology. On the weekends, they'd arrive at Buzzard's Point and be turned over to me. Their translator did not come with them but my Polish was close enough to their Russian for us to get by.

When the Russians discovered that my mother and father had been prisoners of Stalin's, they fell in love with me. We had a wonderful time. Whatever I asked them to do, they did. They even made a game of getting my wood stocks ready for the winter, racing each other in an attempt to see who could cut down the most trees in one day. The trees they cut cleared one side of our future lake bed.

As a funny aside, we also had a team of West German executives over a couple months later. During the week, they'd be in Ohio reviewing Don's latest machines, and on the weekends, they'd be with us. We got them to clear some of the trees on the other side of the lake. Unlike the Russians, who had enjoyed the physical exertion, the Germans had no interest in becoming manual laborers. They would try to hide from Wheeler, but ultimately to no avail. It was ironic to me that people from the two nations that had oppressed my parents, and my people, were the ones to clear our land. How times change.

This being the Cold War, a member of the KGB had made the trip with the Russian engineers. He was there to insure that nobody got the idea of seeking political asylum. The engineers were as warm and raucous as their guard was solemn and suspicious.

We had a number of three-wheel drive vehicles we used to transport ourselves over our land. One day, we gave one to each of the engineers and suddenly, in the middle of the Pennsylvania countryside, they each roared off in their own direction. The KGB agent was livid and beside himself as he tried to decide who to follow and how to get them all back. We howled, as he raced around in utter turmoil.

In August 1975, we were ready for our first guests. The infrastructure was in place, without a bit of assistance by the city, which was just the way Wheeler wanted it. We opened our gates and the people flowed in.

Buzzard's Point-Silver Valley was a hit from day one. Our cabins were rented out, the conference center was in constant use, and the restaurant I'd opened, was packed. It was such a success, that we bought an additional 100 acres of land and started planning for a year round community, that we would call Rocky Ridge Village.

Our second summer started off with a bang. On America's Bicentennial birthday, July 4, 1976, we hosted a huge party at the resort. We had bands, food, races on the lake, balloons, beer and at night a spectacular fireworks display. The event was a brilliant success and Buzzard's Point-Silver Valley was becoming well known. We ran ads in the New Yorker magazine and this added to the awareness. Things were going so well, that we accelerated the pace of the work on Rocky Ridge Village and started talking about a second development in South Carolina.

The reality was that during this time, work was my reality. We were putting up 130 houses in Rocky Ridge Village and in effect building our own town, complete with roads, utilities and its own water tower. I'd wake up with plans on my mind. The business was all that I thought about. Our dinners were board meetings and our lunches were quick breaks on the back of bulldozers. The work was great, but the personal problems I'd been noticing, continued to worsen. Periodic visits from Wheeler's kids deepened my disdain for the way he dealt with his family. As the victim of a horribly dysfunctional family, I was particularly sensitive to the effect he was having on the kids.

I watched, horrified, as he would tell his children vicious lies about their mother. He was cold-heartedly doing everything he could to hurt her relationship with them. I did like one of Wheeler's sons, Michael, who visited on a regular basis. I had no real relationship with any of his other children, who were seldom invited to visit.

37

"V" IS FOR VICIOUS
(1977)

Our fights began to spread into new areas. I had never asked Don for a child, too consumed and content with our business-based relationship and I knew that Don's existing seven children were already more than he ever wanted. Even so, I was surprised one night when he asked me to have my tubes tied. I thought about it and decided to see a doctor.

He confirmed what I was already thinking, that such a procedure was ill advised. Tying one's tubes constituted significant surgery that could have complicated side effects. Besides, I was still young and one never knew what the future may bring. Meanwhile, a vasectomy was a minor out patient procedure that would only cause a day or two's worth of discomfort for Don.

I went back to Don and told him that the doctor wouldn't even do the operation knowing that Wheeler could take care of the issue in a much safer and easier manner. Wheeler wasn't happy but he agreed to have the vasectomy done, and in March, 1977, he went in and got "snipped".

I imagine many doctors would say that what happened to Don next was more psychological than physiological, but in either case, as soon as Don had his vasectomy, he became a changed man. Unfortunately, it was not a change for the better.

Whether for physical or mental reasons, after the surgery, Don Wheeler became a different person. Suddenly, there was nothing I could do right. If I wasn't with him, he'd be angry I wasn't there. When I was with him, he'd be angry that I wasn't in the restaurant working, or tending to some other part of our business. He became a quieter and darker version of himself. If I did or said anything he didn't like, Wheeler would bring down a wall of silence between us and just cut me out of his world.

He began to openly resent the attention I continued to receive from the press and the business community in Franklin. He hated the fact that I would call him on his abhorrent treatment of his family. He became suspicious of my actions and jealous of any man that dared speak to me. Eventually his behavior became so severe, that he began to remind me of my father.

Still, the resort was continuing to grow and the pace with which we had to work, did not allow for time to reflect on personal problems. As troubled as I was with Wheeler's behavior, I was thrilled with our business success. I was running a resort, building homes, managing a restaurant, doing the books for multiple companies, driving once a week to Ohio and doing it all with a smile. I found life exhilarating. The more work there was, the happier I was.

After the vasectomy, Don became very protective of his ownership of all our businesses. The more I helped make Buzzard's Point-Silver Valley profitable, the angrier Don became. Even though he had managed to keep most everything in his name, I was on the books with some ownership of stock, and there were also six homes, in Rocky Ridge Village, that I held title to. He started to see me as less of a partner and more of a threat. I was the one person in his life who could potentially tear part of his empire away. I still thought I could get Wheeler to see that I remained his loving wife and not a threat, but in the end, you can't train wolves.

By the time the summer ended, and we started to close things up for the winter, our personal relationship was as cold and gray as the Pennsylvania weather. We were basically on autopilot, focused on the building and the plans for the new South Carolina project.

Wheeler was already preparing to go to South Carolina, at the head of a convoy of trucks, hauling our equipment, so he could start work on the new resort. While he drove there, I would fly home and use the time to figure out how to get our marriage working again. Little did I know what would happen, once I got there.

38

A PROCLAMATION

I knew I could use the time in London to unwind and figure out what in the world had happened to our relationship. At this point, I thought I was still in love with Don and that his aberrant behavior was just that: an aberration. I believed that the Don Wheeler I had met would reappear and things would return to normal. We just needed to get away from each other and let a little time pass.

The day of my flight, Don drove me to the airport. Neither of us said more than a word or two, the entire way. We arrived at the airport and discovered that waiting for me at the gate, was the mayor of Franklin, the head of the chamber of commerce and a reporter from the newspaper.

Unbeknownst to either of us, the city was in hot pursuit of an English company that was looking to open a subsidiary in America. The mayor was designating me as the person whose job it was to make sure that subsidiary ended up in Franklin.

The mayor handed me a formal letter of invitation and told me there were meetings scheduled the next week in London. After the work they'd seen me do at Buzzard's Point-Silver Valley, they had no qualms in putting their faith in me. The fact I was heading to London, on my own dime, only made my service that much more appealing.

As I agreed to give it my best, I looked past the reporters and for a moment I gazed directly into Wheelers eyes. They were dark with resentment and he returned my gaze with an icy cold stare. It caused me to draw my breath and in that moment I knew that our relationship had just entered dangerous territory.

I had a premonition that to continue living with Wheeler would be fraught with peril. I was somewhat ambivalent about it actually, as Don's behavior with me, his children, his first wife and even his mother, was boorish, and I was sick of it. However, I was not just his wife, I was his business partner and I still held out hope that our life together was salvageable.

A few moments later, I was hustled on board the plane. I crumpled into my seat, looked at the mayor's proclamation and closed my eyes, with a sigh.

39

BETRAYED AGAIN

When we landed at Heathrow Airport, I grabbed a taxi and went to see my parents. The next evening the phone rang. My mother answered it and quickly handed it to me. I took the phone and said "hello." On the other end of the line was Wheeler. I remember to this day the cold steel in his voice as he said one line and then hung up; "Our marriage is over and all you have are the clothes you are wearing." I stood there stunned. My mother later told me that she could actually see the blood drain out of my face, leaving me a ghostly white. I knew Don well enough to know that it truly was over, having seen him do the same thing to his mother, ex-wife and child.

My mother asked what was wrong as I reached for a chair and sat down. I had known that our marriage was rocky, but I never thought he would do what he had just done. You just don't end a life together with one cold statement over the phone. I was assuming he would come to his senses and we'd get to work on the South Carolina project which promised to be even a bigger success than our first resort. However, I was wrong. In one moment, I had gone from being a married wealthy entrepreneur to a separated unemployed pauper.

The next morning, I called the American Embassy and asked for a reference. I needed a law firm that could handle my case. By the next day, I had lawyers on board. There were no pretenses in my mind; I knew that this was going to be a war.

Over the next two months, there were two things that became abundantly clear: one was that the man Don Wheeler had become was an absolute bastard and the other was that he had learned his lessons well. Having gone through one savage divorce, Don Wheeler was ready to give it to me with both barrels.

We were married in Las Vegas, had lived in Pennsylvania and had just bought property in South Carolina. The result was that Wheeler's attorneys could keep shifting the venue for the divorce from one jurisdiction to the next. The fact that I was in England made things more difficult, as well. On top of all this, Wheeler had assets spread out across companies and countries all around the world.

This was 1977 and women were not automatically awarded hoards of money, especially when being divorced by someone as devious and insidious as Don Wheeler. I knew I was fighting a losing battle, but I was damned if I was going to go down without a fight. One unwanted victory came a year or two later when I learned that without me there to run it, Buzzard's Point-Silver Valley had already collapsed and the conference center, restaurant and resort were closed. Though it was confirmation, as to the role I played in the success we'd shared, I could not help but feel sad.

40

THE WALLS COME CRASHING DOWN

In England, the emotional toll was starting to wear on me. I was back in my parent's home and remarkably; again I had to fight Zygmunt off of me. I would push him away when he'd try and give me a big hug and I treated him with the cold disdain he deserved. His response was to tell me that my marriage was over because I had obviously done something wrong. It must have been my fault.

My mother was sympathetic but unable to help me in the battle I was now engaged in. I was having a hard time coming to grips with the fact that the project I had spent five years of my life on, was suddenly ripped away from me. The thought that I was no longer a key part of Buzzard's Point-Silver Valley and Rocky Ridge Village was devastating.

With the stress of the divorce, my insomnia worsened. If I was able to sleep for two hours, it was a good night. I began losing weight and my health began to suffer. Wheeler's betrayal was breaking me down.

In December, my attorney informed me that Wheeler had asked that I fly back to South Carolina so we could try to work things out. I was wary of what Wheeler was up to, but in the back of my head, I wanted to believe that his behavior would change and he would go back to being the man I had married. I agreed to fly back and meet with him, but first, I was going to stop in Pennsylvania and gather a number of my things, including my dog.

A few days later, I landed and headed out to Buzzard's Point. When I got there, I found that the gas had been turned off in our home. I would have no heat while I stayed there, other than from the fireplace. It was sunken into the ground with sofas built around it, so the heat radiated out and kept me quite warm. The first day I was there, I went to the bank only to discover that all of our bank accounts had been emptied. I couldn't withdraw a penny. A month earlier I had been a rich woman, suddenly I was a pauper.

When I returned to our home, I discovered that most of my files, and valuables, had been removed. I went to our vehicle shed and found that the wheels themselves had been taken off of every car we owned. It was clear that Wheeler was taking no chances. I went back to my house and found the door open. I went inside, finding my clothes strewn around my bedroom and my jewelry missing. Things began to feel quite ominous.

I sat down by the fireplace trying to figure out how to deal with the situation. With the phone cut off, I had no one to talk to and nowhere to go. Our house was a half-mile from the gate and there was snow on the unplowed roads. I finally fell asleep by the fire.

I was woken later that night by the cracking retort of a gun and the sound of shattering glass. I leapt up and by firelight; I saw a hole in the wall a little bit above where I'd been sleeping. A bullet had lodged itself there.

I ran into a room that had no windows and lay on the floor with the lights off. I stayed that way until morning; fearing the shooter would come in for a second shot. As soon as the sun was up, I drove to the front gatehouse and called the police. They came out, but all they could do was tell me I was lucky the bullet had missed. There were no clues that they could find, no witnesses and no suspects.

Though I had no proof, in my heart, I was sure that the gunman had been paid by a dark and dangerous man down in South Carolina, and that's where I was going to go, to have it out with him. I may have been scared by the things that were happening, but I wasn't afraid of Don Wheeler. Nobody was going to treat me this way and get away with it.

41

THE FINAL BLOW

Wheeler picked me up at the airport and didn't even pretend he was happy to see me. His first words are still imprinted on my mind, "I have talked to a lawyer and I know exactly what I can and cannot say to you. There is no way we can get back together because you are too ambitious and I am over the hill." I stared at him with continued astonishment, as he went on to add; "The lawyer said that I must tell you, you can come back to me. But, if you do, I will not allow you to work for me or for anyone else. The only thing we will ever discuss is the weather."

I asked him how I was expected to live, and he responded, "I'll give you a few dollars a week, and that is all. No car!" He barely said another word, as he stared straight ahead and focused on driving. Eventually, he offered me another alternative: "The only other option is for you to accept a divorce." He went on to lay out his draconian terms. "I'll give you $15,000, paid out over three years, and not a penny more." We turned off on an old road and headed far out into the countryside, as I sat there stunned by the audacity of his offer. Buzzard's Point-Silver

Valley alone was worth millions of dollars, and I had built it with him, brick by brick.

We came to a silent stop in front of a trailer, in the middle of nowhere. I hauled my own bag out of the truck and dragged it inside. Before I knew what he was doing, Wheeler closed the door and left. I was in an isolated trailer with no car, no food and no phone. I was trapped and stranded. I had no idea which way to walk and the temperature was hovering just above freezing. If I got lost, I wouldn't survive the night.

I was exhausted, so I sat down and cursed the man who had just dropped me off. Finally, I fell asleep. Hours later, well after dark, I heard a truck driving up. Moments later, Don opened the front door and came towards me. He grabbed my arm and pushed me into a bedroom, where he proceeded to rape me.

I could pretend that there was some part of it that was consensual, but there wasn't. He overpowered me and did his best to demonstrate to me that he was in control. In those days, there was no judge that would have put him in jail for what he did; after all, we were still legally married. Yet, he raped me as sure as I am here writing this.

The next night, he again forced himself upon me. The next morning, Wheeler wouldn't stop telling me I was stupid for thinking I had any right to his money. He spoke in a cold calculated manner that made me feel as if I'd never really known him. By the middle of the third day, I feared for my life. There was no more doubt in my mind, I was sure that Wheeler was the one responsible for the gunshot. My health was breaking down quickly. The lack of sleep and food were weighing heavily on me.

Wheeler's $15,000 offer was ludicrous, but I knew I had to get out of the trailer and away from him, before he went completely crazy and killed me. I finally told him I thought his deal sounded fair. "Draw up the papers" I said.

Proud of himself, Wheeler put me in his truck and took me into the nearest town for a meal. When he went into the bathroom, I raced for a pay phone and called my attorney in London, collect. He answered the phone and I told him what was going on. He told me, I was right to agree to anything Wheeler wanted, whatever it took to get away from him. We'd get out of it later.

I jumped back into my seat at our table, just before Wheeler returned. We drove back to the trailer and that night he let me sleep in peace. First though, Wheeler called our attorney, in Franklin, and dictated to him the terms, he'd thrust down my throat. I knew that Wheeler had a big meeting in South Carolina the next day. Using my female guile, I convinced Wheeler to send me, back to Franklin on my own, so I could sign the papers, before I had to be back in England.

Wheeler looked me up and down with a cold calculated look. Obviously, he felt that he'd broken me. A grim smile played along one side of his mouth and he told me to get cleaned up. His arrogance was such that he truly believed that I had given in to his impossible demands. An hour later, we were headed towards the airport again. When I got out of his truck, I literally ran to the plane.

I didn't breathe, until the wheels lifted off from the tarmac. As soon as I got to Franklin, I went to the attorney who Wheeler had called. I raced into his office with a story prepared, about how I'd come back in on Monday, to sign the papers. I had to buy time to get my things and get out of town. However, the attorney beat me to the punch, telling me that he couldn't believe the way Wheeler was treating me. I told him that the terms were fine and that I would come back on Monday, but of course I had no intention of returning. I just wanted to make sure he would say that everything was fine, if Don called him.

The attorney looked at me with an odd expression on his face. I looked at my reflection in a mirror on his wall and barely recognized myself. My complexion was sickly pale, bags were under my eyes and my hair hung limp. I looked as if I was either just coming out of, or just going into, the hospital.

I excused myself and drove back to my house. I collapsed on the bed, only to be awakened a few minutes later, by a knock on the front door. I jumped up, looking for something to defend myself with, when I heard a familiar voice.

A good friend of mine, named Sandy, had come looking for me, having heard that I was back in town as well as rumors that Don and I were getting a divorce. She took one look at me and pushed me into her truck. On the way to her home, I told her everything that was going on.

Sandra wasn't a city girl. She was from hardy Pennsylvania stock. She drove a pickup and carried a rifle on the gun rack behind her seat. We went to her home and drew up my escape plan. I had clothes, pictures and a few papers, that Wheeler hadn't found, and I was not going back to England without them. The next morning we made a trip into town and filled the back of her truck with boxes.

Sandra and I then headed down the road towards Buzzard's Point. Before we got to the main gate, we veered off road and literally drove through the forest. We plummeted down the mountain, plowing through the three foot deep snow, and crossing two frozen streams, while we watched for signs we'd been seen. I had the gun on my lap, just in case. We almost went over the side of the trail, a couple times, but after a half hour we came up behind my home. We opened and closed the doors as quietly as possible and headed in through the back door.

We had no idea if the gunman was still out there waiting for me to return. I flew from room to room grabbing everything that had any kind of sentimental value to me. We threw the last of the boxes into the back of the truck and after just forty-five minutes, we were about to head out, when I realized there was one additional thing I had to do.

During my years at Buzzard's Point we'd always kept a pack of dogs. Two of them in particular were mine. One: a beautiful Weimaraner, had died that summer; but my other dog, a Newfoundland named Tarzan, had come racing into the house shortly after we'd arrived. He'd heard the car and instantly sensed I was back.

I couldn't leave Tarzan behind. I jumped out of the truck and loaded him into the back with the boxes. I got back in and looked at Sandra who agreed on the spot to take care of my dog for me. With that settled, we set out on our getaway.

We couldn't go out the way we'd come in, as we'd most likely get stuck in the snow, now that we'd be going up, instead of downhill. We looked at each other and decided to make a run for it, right out the main gate, using the main road. I gripped the gun a little tighter, as Sandra gunned it.

We roared through the middle of the empty resort. I was anticipating somebody jumping out to stop us, at any moment. As we approached the gate, I hit the remote and to my great relief the gate swung open. We flew past the caretaker's house and five minutes later, we were on the highway, headed for the airport.

It was right about that moment, when I hit my limit and began descending into a dark pit. Sandra threw the boxes through the door of the shipping company and then had to nearly carry me to the gate at the airport. By the time I boarded the plane, I had no more energy. When the wheels finally touched down in England, I was almost comatose. Finally, as the cab stopped in front of my parent's home, I stayed slumped over in the back seat, lacking the strength to get out by myself.

My mother rushed out and helped lift me out of the cab. The next thing I remember is waking up a day later, too weak to get out of bed. My mind and body had completely collapsed.

Five years and a million pounds of stress came crashing down upon me. The betrayal, the heartbreak and the sorrow competed with the anger, for the foremost position in my mind. I drifted in and out of consciousness. Later, I discovered that a doctor had come in every other day to check on me, of his own volition. When he did so, my mother would have to turn me over for him, as I lacked the strength and often the consciousness to do so. When I finally woke up, even the simplest task of writing a letter was beyond my capacity. It would take me three months before I'd be able to again start functioning, somewhat normally.

Don Wheeler had come very close to killing me, however, in my darkest hour; my mother's healing hands were there to nurture me back to health. Though she had missed so many opportunities to be a true mother, in this instance she was there. My father continued to berate me for losing another husband, but his voice had long ago lost its power over me.

42

BACK TO WORK
(1978)

It took the winter for me to recover. I remember a friend coming over and telling me I was so thin, that I looked like a coat hanger. Finally, by April, I was again able to function. It was right at this time, that I contacted an old friend. Brian Kent took my call and after I told him I was back in London, and looking for work, he offered me the position of PR Manager, on the spot. This time I would even get a company car.

Alfa-Laval had changed during my five-year absence. There were a 'few' more women in positions of power and the blatant sexism of before, seemed to have been ratcheted down a notch. Ron was still there; at least part of the time.

More than a few people came up to me, expressing their relief that I was back. I threw myself back into work and focused on getting things back up to snuff. I was thrilled to have something positive in my life and my health improved dramatically.

After a short time, I noticed that Brian was not as engaged, as he had been before. The reason soon became clear. He was leaving Alfa-Laval to join a multi-national consortium, which did business around the globe. Brian was moving on to something extra-ordinary.

I thought of staying on, but decided that I was so identified with Brian, that I'd be looked at with a touch of suspicion by the new President. I had no worries about finding further employment. I was fully recovered from my breakdown and there was no shortage of companies that would want a person with my experience.

After my work at Buzzard's Point and a second stint with Brian, I was a businesswoman who knew how to make things happen. My batteries were recharged and I was back in charge of my life. It was time to go find something new to do.

43

STAR WARS

It was early summer, in 1978, when Brian left for Stavely Industries. Soon thereafter, a corporate headhunter tracked me down and within a short time; I was running the film and television division of a massive prop and furniture rental company called Giltspur Furnishing Hire.

The English film production business had recently been reignited by George Lucas and his "Star Wars" trilogy. The James Bond movies were also enjoying global success, and in general, it was a boom time for the movie business in London. Giltspur was benefiting from this renaissance, but they had lost a very large account at the BBC and they wanted it back.

A week after I started, I walked into the office of the person who had cancelled the account, and told them that Giltspur was under new management, and I was that management. I returned to my new office with the account in hand. From that moment on, I could do no wrong. The president of the company grew to love me more, as I began turning our treasure trove of props into, well... treasure.

The first thing that leapt out at me was the incredible number of paintings that were stacked on top of each other, so you could not see any of them. The men seemed astonished at the concept of hanging up the paintings, but I made them do it. It turns out we had the largest painting collection in the business. We were able to get thousands of our 20,000-piece collection, up on the walls, and once our clients could see them they started adding them to their orders.

I tended to look at things differently than the men there. Where they saw organized stacks of paintings, I saw a wasted opportunity to better market our wares. The boss loved the way I looked at things.

In my overhaul of the warehouse, we came across two antique bronze cherubs. I rang a friend who worked at Sotheby's, and he came back with a price he believed they'd fetch at auction. I told him to put them on the docket and I quickly had copies made. We sold the originals for six figures. The replicas were more popular than ever now that we could say they were identical to antiques that had recently sold at auction for a small fortune.

I combed through every prop we had, when the Star Wars' team came in. We ended up customizing a beautiful glass and crystal waterfall for a wonderful shot in the third Star Wars film. The BBC was keeping us very busy and I was constantly meeting with movie directors and prop masters. It was different from anything I'd done before, but at this point, I understood that business was business. Two people who could help each other profit, were smart to do so.

During this time, I acquired another Weimaraner. I loved my dog and I took him to work with me on a daily basis. One of the starchy execs from corporate objected, but I didn't care. I knew what I was worth to the president of the company, and if I wanted my dog, I knew I could keep my dog. I was right. During the day, he'd run around the grounds with the gardener, who loved him.

So much of business is vision, what you see and what others see. I made sure people who looked at me saw a woman, who was very well put together, and in charge of every situation. Wherever I looked, I saw opportunity: both professionally and personally. I was in my mid-thirties, my health was good again and my heart was unencumbered by any deviant relationships. I had no interest in becoming serious with anyone, especially as I was still involved with ongoing legal matters with Wheeler and his legal wrecking crew.

Times were stark in England, as a malaise had set in. Yet, in depressed times, entertainment tends to do well and in the late 70's nothing was bigger than the movies we were making in England. The Star Wars films had set off a cavalcade of effects-filled pictures with lavish sets, and as a result, our business thrived.

I was there for a little over a year. They loved me at Giltspur and I had a future there, though the disparity in salaries for men and women remained disturbing. The one problem I had in my life was my ongoing divorce proceedings with Don Wheeler.

SKIRMISHES

While I was busy rebuilding my life, Wheeler and his dynamite attorneys were building a false case against me, complete with hidden assets, imagined infidelity and forged affidavits. Wheeler had actually filed the divorce in Las Vegas, so the court would know nothing about his true assets. The correspondence between our attorneys was wicked. He was accusing me of everything under the sun.

Mind you, all this was coming from a man who had kidnapped and assaulted me. He was painting himself the victim and I vowed to make things as difficult as I could for him. I would not be cowed by this bull. I stood my ground. However, my ground felt like quicksand.

I did have a few arrows in my quiver, however. My name was alone on the title of six modular homes that we'd installed at Rocky Ridge Village. When I left for England, all six of the homes were rented out and producing income. Within a year they were the only six homes in Rocky Ridge that were empty.

On top of that Wheeler was sending me bogus bills for repairs that were neither done, nor needed.

I called the attorney, who had covered for me when I was trying to escape Wheeler, and I asked him for his help. A couple days later, a series of trucks, pulled into the village, complete with a court order, giving them the power to disassemble the homes and cart them away to auction. I was told that Wheeler went through the roof. I can imagine him standing there, beside himself with anger, as six of his homes were driven off. I would have liked to be a fly on one of the walls, on that day.

I knew that in the end, he held too many cards for me to win. For one thing, the attorneys I'd been referred to were corporate attorneys, not specialists in divorce. For another, I'd have to hire a separate set of attorneys and forensic accountants in each state and country he had assets hidden. Even so, I was enjoying causing him whatever angst I could. Bigger showdowns were coming but after the homes were sold, our divorce proceedings actually slowed down.

In March, 1978, Wheeler called me and asked to see me, so I could sign our last tax return together. I had no intention of signing anything that Wheeler wanted me to, but I did want to play with him in any way I could. I told Wheeler I'd be happy to sign the returns, but I wasn't going to be back in the States for a few months and he'd have to come to London.

Wheeler agreed and flew over the next week. I told him to meet me in a public place. We sat down together just long enough for me to tell him he was a criminal and I hoped he'd enjoyed his flight. His face turned red with fury as I stood up and walked away, without having signed a thing. That was the last time I ever spoke to Don Wheeler.

45

BACK WITH BRIAN
(1979)

The money from my houses paid for a nice flat in London that I soon settled into. In the summer of 1979, my mother called and told me that my old boss had called for me. Brian was settled into Stavely Industries and with eighty companies to oversee, he wanted the help of an old friend, me.

Stavely Industries had been a wealthy steel company that had to reinvent itself when England nationalized the steel industry, years before. With no business, but mountains of cash, Stavely started buying up companies. By the time they were done, eighty new businesses had been sewn together into one massive portfolio. Brian Kent had been brought in as a company director and would progress through the roles of president, CEO and ultimately, chairman of the company, before he was through.

After getting the message, I called his office. Brian jumped right on the line. "Basia", he said, "I want you to be one of my directors". It took me but the blink of an eye to respond, "Yes".

I gave my notice at Giltspur the next day, and a month later, I started at Stavely Industries.

My official title was Communications Director. I would oversee all contact with the press and media. On top of that, I would produce the yearly report, which included in depth sections on each company. This meant that I'd have to become intimately familiar with the principal players from every company. I'd also need to get a grasp of where each company's strengths and weaknesses lay.

When I started work, I could see that as much as Brian needed competent people around him, he also needed a friend he could talk to. I was the only person that Brian brought over from Alfa-Laval and I was honored by his trust.

The companies that Stavely owned were all established businesses that shared a common need. They needed to enter the modern world of business, communication and technology. They also needed to improve relations between labor and management.

Brian believed that productivity and profitability would be improved quite a bit if his companies implemented more advanced and evolved communication protocols. His directors were in charge of introducing these protocols to the companies they oversaw. Brian wanted people in his companies to do the unthinkable, "Talk to each other". He put me in charge of indoctrinating the most stubborn companies.

Stavely had companies in England, America, Australia, Denmark and Canada, but a company headquartered in Manchester, England stood out as the most resistant of all. The management and labor did not speak - period. The managers were medieval-thinking snobs and the laborers were basically flaming communist revolutionaries, ready to burn the building down, if they didn't get their way. They felt management was a waste of time as they could manage themselves. Of course, one can instantly see the problem with that logic.

Manchester is a 'hard knocks' city where life is tough and the people tougher. I walked into that hornets' nest with a briefcase full of nifty charts and a speech that I was worried would not go over well. It didn't! Five minutes into my presentation, they started heckling me. When it came to receiving and sharing my message, they were deaf and dumb, with the emphasis on dumb.

In effect, they saw me as a city girl trying to come into their town and take their jobs away. I made it through my presentation to the men on the day shift, but the men on the night shift were in no mood for my fancy foolishness. Shortly after starting my speech, I could see that if I finished it, the men might finish me. I asked for a short break and walked out... of the building.

Aside from the days I was on the verge of getting mugged, I was having a fantastic time at Stavely Industries. Brian was grooming me to be the first female president of one of their smaller companies; Salter Housewares, which had about sixty employees. Small though it may be, what Brian was planning was a huge step for me and every other woman in the company. In all of England, there were but a handful of female presidents. It just wasn't done.

Brian had no patience for such antiquated thinking and only cared that I could help him make the company succeed. I was on the path to heights, I could have never imagined back in my days at boarding school. Brian had mentored me for over three years, between my two stints at Alfa-Laval and now at Stavely. He saw that I was ready to take on much more and he was right. It just wouldn't turn out to be with him. Circumstances were about to point me back towards America.

46

GLOBE TROTTING
(1980)

Stavely was a massive company and I was constantly on the road visiting one company or another. While the British tax code was notorious for ripping every last pound from a person's purse, at that time, it was as lax as could be, when it came to expense accounts. Hence, my lunches and dinners at the Savoy and Annabele's were back on the docket.

I was entertaining business people constantly. Whenever the president of one of our subsidiaries came in, we treated them like royalty. One such person was Peter Stanton, president of a company called Electroscales, which I had first visited on a business trip to California. Peter had thought I'd hit it off with his wife and when he next came to London he brought her along. He was right, we hit it off. Her name was Andrea, and she was a character right out of central casting.

Andrea Stanton was a strikingly beautiful woman, with the heart of a showgirl. She commanded a room from the moment she made her entrance. Any man, entering a room, attracted her attention until she attracted his. For three days she and I hit the town. We'd head out to see the crown jewels, spend five minutes looking at them, and then make a bee line to a top restaurant where we'd hold court for hours.

Though she was married, Andrea enjoyed the attention of men and she got it. On our three-day soirée, my brother became part of our entourage and I think he too fell under Andrea's spell for a night. By the end of Andrea's visit, we had assembled quite a crowd and our last evening went on into early hours of the next day.

During our time together, I discovered that Andrea had an artistic side. It turned out that she was a sought after decorator back home. Listening to her talk about the projects she was in the middle of, I realized how much I missed having my own company. I missed being in charge. By the time Andrea and Peter headed home, she and I had become fast friends. As they walked to the plane, I promised to come see them that summer.

In the interim, I was going all over the globe, visiting the various Stavely subsidiaries. Some were in major cities, where I could enjoy my stay in a five star hotel. Many of the companies, however, were in out of the way places, where my hotels were apt to have drunken salesmen yelling in the corridors. In places like that, I began to dream about going back to America.

47

MY EVENINGS WITH BRIAN

When I wasn't out on the road, I was most likely clocking long hours at the office. Brian also worked long hours and at night he would come into my office. After everyone else had gone, we would talk about business and about life. I so greatly valued Brian's words of advice. He helped me better process my thoughts, as I started to think about what I really wanted to do next.

Brian was a remarkable business man and during these conversations he would share his work philosophy with me. His principles stay with me to this day. When I am asked for my secret to success I quickly respond "hard work." There is no substitute for working hard. There is also no substitute for having the courage to put your thoughts into action. Once you decide to do something it is imperative that you make a plan and then put everything you have into it. Perhaps most importantly, once you start implementing your plan, never give up. Circumstances may combine to stop you but never stop yourself.

During this time the English economy was in bad shape. The government set up a trust to educate the ministers about business and likewise educate British businessmen, as to how the government worked. Every large company was assigned two ministers, one Labor and one Conservative. It was my job to take care of the ministers assigned to Stavely.

I traveled the country with them, introducing them to the presidents and managers of our various companies. I found the Labor Minister, Renee Short, to be fascinating. We had long conversations about the state of the country as we criss-crossed England. The other minister, assigned to our company, struck me as a buffoon and if he ever said anything worth listening to, I missed it.

Brian was a great believer in education and he was invited by a professor at Oxford to put five of his top executives into an intensive management course they were putting on. I was one of the five Stavely executives that attended the course.

One of the events, I attended during this time was a luncheon at Cambridge University, attended by about fifty people. One of those in attendance was the Duke of Edinburgh, the Queen's husband, who was the patron of Cambridge's Kings College, which was the host college for the course and luncheon. I was sitting at a table near the front when he walked in. As the Duke passed me, he swung around and looked back, staring directly at me.

I knew a look of interest when I saw one, and I immediately realized that I had caught the Duke's eye. After lunch, I was standing by myself, when the Duke walked into the room, his security detail flanking him, on either side. I saw him say something to them and they walked out of the room. The moment they were out of sight, the Duke wheeled around and walked directly over to me.

As he approached, I couldn't help but noticing that he looked a great deal like my father. Such thoughts left my mind as soon as he began talking to me. He had a natural charm that was instantly appealing. I was just beginning to wonder where this conversation was going to lead, when his security detail returned. I saw them look around the room and as soon as they saw the Duke, they hurried over, and shuffled him off. He gave me a sly smile and then was gone.

Brian and I would share stories such as these at night, laughing and sometimes swearing about the things that would happen to us. During these sessions, I'd pitch stories to Brian for the company magazine, which I was also in charge of. I was a perpetual motion machine that he kept fueled with new tasks.

Brian had a profound effect on me, probably more than he knows. He was the first man in my life that made me believe in myself. He helped me realize that if I wanted to, I could do anything. Later on in life, his words would keep me going through some very challenging times. Right now my nightly chats were the perfect way to cap my days.

When I wasn't working, I was having fun with a gentleman friend, seeing good friends or reading my beloved books, while listening to my music. The only thing that was still causing me trouble was my divorce from Don Wheeler.

BEATING THE ODDS IN VEGAS

When I was on the road, Brian let me spend whatever I needed, to get the job done. Because I was executing policy designed to make the company millions, I was allowed thousands. I flew first class around the world and stayed in the finest hotels. This was a heady time.

This type of mobility was something that Don Wheeler was not counting on, as he pushed our divorce through the courts. Wheeler had finally filed our divorce in Las Vegas. He did this because he never thought I'd have the where-with-all to make it to court.

It just so happened that the court date we'd been assigned, aligned with a trip I had to make to a company of ours in Seattle. I showed up in court, to the utter astonishment of Wheeler's attorney. The day before, Wheeler had literally shown up in overalls. His testimony painted me as a European gold digger who was trying to take a poor innocent country boy for all he was worth.

If I hadn't shown up, his ruse might have worked, but I not only made it there, I came with newspaper articles, pictures and documents I'd manage to save. Wheeler had flown out the night before, after giving a fraudulent deposition. After I finished, his attorney was caught in a series of lies, which made him look like either an incompetent fool or a corrupt villain.

By the time I was done, the judge was ready to strip Wheeler of everything he'd ever owned. Back in England, I was informed that the judge had ruled in my favor, and awarded Buzzard's Point-Silver Valley to me. I was thrilled for a moment, but I knew it was too good to be true.

Sure enough, a month later my attorney received word that the Las Vegas court had lost jurisdiction on the divorce. Having expected that this would happen, all I could do was to keep fighting and take some solace in the fact that I was making things hard for Wheeler.

49

THE TRUTH WILL SET YOU FREE

Aside from Wheeler, things were continuing to go well and my travels continued. I was packing for a fast four-day trip to Denmark, when I got a call from my mother. I had been at my parent's house earlier that day and had left surprised by how nice my father had been to me. On the phone however, my mother told me that Zygmunt had said some terrible things about me after I'd left. The fact that she could even repeat such lies to me made me furious. I couldn't believe that after all this time, I still had to defend myself to my mother.

Something inside of me snapped. I couldn't pretend any longer. I felt that my mother had to be told and I had to know: had she realized what was going on? If not, how in God's name, had she not known what was happening to her daughter, right beneath her nose?

In her native Polish, I asked my mother if she had any idea what Zygmunt had done to me? Did she know of the abuse I had suffered? I stopped talking and there was silence on the other end of the line. Not wanting to push my mother any further, and feeling quite emotional, I said goodbye and hung up the phone. The next day I flew to Denmark and met with high level executives about low level sprinkler systems.

When I got back to London, and walked into my home my brother was waiting, with a sad look on his face. He told me that we had to go to the hospital. That morning Karolina had suffered a stroke and was now in a coma.

We left immediately and raced to the hospital. When I saw her laying there my heart almost stopped. No one passing in the hall would look in and guess that this woman had flirted with assassins and fought for her country. She looked so small, so old and so weak. Her complexion was lifeless and her breath was shallow. I sat down and took her hand in mine.

Two hours after I got there, I suddenly felt my mother's hand squeeze mine. I looked up and for just a moment, my mother sat up in bed and looked at me with complete clarity. Her eyes let me know that she was desperate to talk to me but she fell back before the words ever came. Perhaps she wanted to beg for my forgiveness, or maybe she wanted to explain how she never knew.

My words had forced my mother to face what she had to have at least suspected was happening in her home. It may be that the only way she could deal with her shame was to leave this life behind. I have always harbored feelings of guilt; that perhaps I should never have mentioned it.

My mother's body would live on for another few months, but her mind would never come back. I would never be able to speak to her again. She was placed in a special ward where she could spend her last little time on earth in peace.

It so happened that I had started dancing again, with the Oscar Kolberg dance company, upon my return to England. In one of the great coincidences of my life, we had been scheduled to perform for the very hospital that my mother was now in.

I approached that evening with mixed emotions. As the night wore on, I found myself taking solace in the movement and the music, just as I always did. We reached the end of the program and I walked out for my final solo. The music started and I began to dance.

Twenty feet away, my mother sat with unseeing eyes, yet somehow I know, that my last dance touched her. I walked away that night with a sad sense of peace. My mother had been far from perfect, but she had survived unspeakable horrors so that her children could be born. In the end, that was her gift to me; life. I told Olga the next day that I was done dancing.

About a week later, the dignified and beautiful spy passed away, still a refugee. A lady to the end, my mother's sacrifice, for her country, will always live on. Ironically, at the same time Karolina left this life, a fledgling freedom movement was emerging in the Polish city of Gdansk. Only a fellow refugee could know just how much it would have meant to her, to have seen Poland free again.

At Karolina's funeral, Zygmunt only wanted to make sure I wasn't going to cut my support payments, now that mother was gone. I simply walked away from him. My father would live another dozen years and his place in my life was not done yet, but at that point, I could stomach none of his poison. I just wanted to get away from him; even being in the same city and country seemed too close.

50

AN INVITATION

After my mother's death I needed to get away. I took Andrea and Peter up on their invitation, and in August 1980, I landed at San Francisco International Airport. Peter and Andrea picked me up and we drove up the coast, over the Golden Gate Bridge and then further north, until we came to the small scenic town of Navato.

For the next three weeks, I soaked in the Californian sun, cuisine and lifestyle. Peter was with us on the weekends, but during the week he stayed in an apartment in the city, to save himself four hours a day of driving. He loved the fact that I had flown to see them. Peter called me an "adventurer" and I could tell that he felt I was a good influence on Andrea.

One day, when we were left to ourselves Andrea shared with me something she'd been thinking about. More and more people had been asking her to decorate their homes. She knew there was a big business opportunity sitting right in front of her. She wanted to start an interior decorating company and she wanted me to be her partner. I was immediately intrigued. I had no doubt that Andrea could generate business. She was a natural salesperson and her energy was extraordinary. Right then and there, I agreed.

For the rest of my stay, we had a wonderful time shopping, sunbathing and visualizing what life would be like when I came to California. I did have some concerns. For example, Andrea was definitely mercurial in nature and I had no doubt that we could have a few conflicts. Still, the prospects for success seemed quite good.

I had another reason for wanting to come to America aside from the incredible Californian climate. In preparing the company's Report and Accounts for the annual shareholders meeting, I had gained access to the corporate salary charts for all of the top executives. I was stunned to discover that Peter and other presidents in America made far more money than Brian Kent. If I ever wanted to make the kind of money I felt I was worth, the place to do it would be in America.

By the time my vacation was over, I couldn't wait to get back. I loved America and since my return to England I had made a point of defending America's honor whenever someone made the mistake of criticizing the USA in my presence. There was a natural optimism in America, that all of its citizens seemed to share. The sky was the limit, whether one was talking about technology, opportunity or access to capital.

When it was time for me to return, we hugged goodbye at the airport and I boarded my plane. As I flew back to my life in London, I could feel myself wanting to turn around and go back to California. When I landed in England I was met by a gray sky and a summer time fog.

America was looking better and better.

51

AMERICA, TAKE TWO

Upon returning, I sensed that Brian was about to name me as president of Salter Housewares. If I didn't tell him immediately, I'd be the president of a company. I knew that once that happened, I'd never be able to walk away. I went into Brian's office and told him of my decision.

Brian was surprised and I think a bit let down. Yet, he could see that I was bound and determined to make it big and he did not wish to stand in my way. I worked for the next three months insuring that the transition was as smooth as could be.

Once I had everything in place, I walked into Brian's office, gave him a hug and thanked him for all he'd done for me. I walked out with a tear in one eye and a sparkle in the other. I was going back to America.

My new adventure started in New York City. Peter, Andrea and her daughter, Electra, thought it would be fun to meet there for Christmas, prior to going back to the west coast. We met at the Plaza Hotel and used it as our base of operations for the next week. My room looked out over Central Park where I could watch the horses pull people on carriages through the trees.

We attended a series of exquisite parties and had a wonderful week in the 'big apple'. From there, we flew to California and Andrea and I began making plans. During our discussions, Andrea shared with me that she and Peter were having trouble in their marriage. Because of this, she wanted to keep the new business quiet, until the divorce was final. Otherwise, the courts could cut her alimony drastically.

I was thrilled to be in California but I was not happy to hear her news. Before we were even started, Andrea was putting limitations on how successful we could become. However, I set my concerns aside as we were still moving forward. The next day we were heading down to L.A. for a series of meetings.

We flew to 'LAX' and went to our hotel in Beverly Hills, where we'd be spending the next five days. We had scheduled meetings with the top architecture and design magazines headquartered there. We knew that one article could generate a huge amount of business and at least I was still interested in nothing less.

The first night in L.A. we were sitting in the bar of the Beverly Wilshire hotel, dressed to the hilt, when a bottle of Dom Perignon was delivered to our table. It had been sent over by a lively Peruvian multi-millionaire who asked if he and his business partner could join us. We invited them to sit down and things were never the same again.

52

CONNIE SANTOS
(1981)

His name was Cornelius (Connie) Santos and he owned an oil distribution company in South America. Connie was bigger than life. In the near future he would buy me seven fur coats in one day, all because a coat of mine had been stolen while in the possession of his chauffer. I would have had a dozen, but I reminded him that I now lived in California and had little need for winter coats. On another occasion he would spend $1,000 on caviar, at lunch with two others, and myself simply because he felt like celebrating life.

Connie Santos was a multi-millionaire who was in the spot oil cargo business. His company would buy huge shipments of oil and then ship it out to the highest bidder. The resulting sales had allowed Connie to build a huge fortune. His business grossed over a billion dollars a year and money seemed to have no meaning to him. From the moment he joined us, everything was on his tab.

Connie was enthralled by the two of us, sitting in the hotel making our plans for our business. I particularly intrigued him, and instantly he asked me to go with him to any place on the planet I wanted. I laughingly turned down the invitation but not the company. We spent hours together talking that first night.

It turned out that Connie was in L.A. looking for someone he could trust to work with him in his latest venture. Connie had managed to secure the output of a number of freshwater shrimp farmers, in his native Peru. There was great demand for shrimp in America and the pipelines needed more product.

The rebel military movement that continues in parts of Peru to this day was terrorizing much of the country in the early 80's. In order to insure he got the shrimp he had contracted for, Connie had provided each facility with armed guards. His farmers were about to start shipping product and he was looking for someone who could handle the sales and marketing in the United States.

Connie Santos needed someone smart, independent, and detail-oriented. He quickly decided that he needed me. That night, out of respect for Andrea, I told him that Andrea and I were partners and I had no time available to help him.

Nevertheless, for the next two days, Connie wined and dined the two of us, in an attempt to change my mind. Still, I refused to break the partnership. Andrea played along, but I could tell that she was not happy. Perhaps she could tell that despite my denials to the contrary, I was quite interested in the opportunity that was being presented to me.

53

SHRIMP, ANYONE?

The day we arrived back at Navato, Andrea told me she had found an apartment for me and told me I should move there immediately. Her demeanor and tone let me know that she was upset that I'd spent so much time talking to Connie about his business. It also let me know that we were better suited as friends than business partners. Instead of driving to see the apartment, I called Connie to make sure his offer still stood. He said it did, and I flew to Southern California. The stretch limo was waiting when I arrived.

In our first meeting, Connie and I worked out the business parameters. I'd open my own distribution company in the States, which I subsequently called Wheeler International. He'd fly the shrimp in to Miami, where I'd have refrigerator trucks waiting to deliver the shrimp to distribution centers in California. Our arrangement was that he'd pay the start up costs and we'd split the profits. I agreed and we shook hands. I told him Wheeler International was open for business.

With Connie, I could make the kind of profits I had come to America for. It would take Andrea a while to get over my departure, but she and I would go on to have more adventures in the future. Andrea would also go on to divorce Peter, further confirming that I had made the right choice.

It is worth noting that in keeping with her flair for the dramatic, Andrea chose Peking (Beijing), China as the city in which she'd leave Peter. She caused a wonderful scene as she stormed out into the streets of a massive city, on the other side of the world. Such a woman, I still love her to death.

With Navato in my past, and tons of shrimp in my future, I landed in L.A. with an optimistic outlook and the need for a new home. My furnishings were still coming on a boat from England so once they hit land; I had them diverted to my new apartment in the den of iniquity, known as Marina Del Rey.

54

MEET ME AT THE MARINA

Marina Del Rey: home to divorced doctors; lawyers; pilots and entrepreneurs; such as yours truly, was an exceptionally fun place to live. I moved into a green oasis called Mariner's Village, which was just a short walk from the water. I stayed there less than a year, but in the months I was there, I made an assortment of great friends. By day, I was selling large amounts of shrimp and by night, I was going to the most extraordinary parties.

I was 37 years old and, mostly due to genetics, my body remained in prime bikini shape. One day, I was lying out at the pool and one of the divorced doctors in our building commented that I was lucky to have genes like mine. He cautioned me that I was at the age where I had to start taking good care of my body, if I had any thoughts of still wearing that bikini a few years down the road.

This simple conversation made a lasting impression on me. I had never worried about nutrition or exercise before. Between my distaste for sweets, my natural physique, love of sports and dancing, I'd never needed to exercise or pay much attention to what I was eating. However, I knew he was right, it was time to educate myself. During my time in the Marina, I began reading about nutrition and I started exercising. Ever since that day at the pool, I have worked out on a regular basis.

It turned out that Andrea was quite knowledgeable about eating healthy foods. She and I began to compare notes. Over time I crafted a few simple dietary and skincare procedures that along with my workouts and some clever work by a plastic surgeon, or two, have kept me on top of my game. By the way, my attitude towards cosmetic surgery is simple. If God hadn't wanted us to use it, he wouldn't have given us doctors with the ability to transfer fat from our butts to our cheeks.

I learned early on, from Dr Lawrence Birnbaum, in Beverly Hills, and later Dr David Wolf, in La Jolla, that the best way to utilize plastic surgery is in cautious moderation. People who think plastic surgery is going to make their problems go away are gravely mistaken. However, it can do wonders for one's self-confidence when utilized correctly. A little bit here and there, every now and then, is the way to do it. With that being said, I now disavow ever having had anything done, or even knowing the doctors mentioned above.

I cannot stress enough how important this 'program' has been in my life. As I grew older, it would help pull me through a very dark and difficult time. For now though, the exercises were a nice tune up that kept me sharp for business and for pleasure. Connie was providing plenty of business and in the Marina there was never a shortage of pleasure.

55

MALIBU

Over the years, my brother had crafted a nice career as an actor, doing films and television, in England. When I made the move to California, he followed me there and fit right into the festivities at the Marina. He still had no seeming sense of exactly how rent worked, but it was nice to have my baby brother with me.

In the Marina, we found a group of good looking, highly paid, revelers living life for all it was worth. There were boat bashes, penthouse parties and hot tub rendezvous'. The Marina's reputation had not been built lightly. There was no shortage of men to meet and corks to pop.

There were six of us who would go on to be dear friends, years after I left the Marina. Andrew and Christina Renner, Olena and Fred Snow, myself and a man that would play a key role in my life, a couple years later, Duncan Barker. We grew close and supported each other when we were up and when we were down. Most of the time we were up, and we celebrated that fact, on an almost daily basis. Yes, the Marina was fun!

After nine months however, I was growing tired of living in Zion, and decided it was time to buy a home. The shrimp business was booming and it was apparent that money was going to be in great supply. The American consumer had an ever-growing appetite for shrimp and Connie and I had tons of the stuff. Our first shipments had sold so quickly that we were already talking about expanding. The money I was being cheated out of by Wheeler, suddenly looked a lot less important.

I started looking for my dream home and I found it in the Pacific Palisades. It was a lovely house with a pool and tennis court, on two acres of lush land. It was located in a gated community that was populated with celebrities such as Chevy Chase and Jane Fonda, who was a frequent visitor to the home next to the one I fell in love with.

I put one hundred thousand dollars down and went into escrow and returned to my Malibu digs to prepare for the move. About three months earlier, when I had first talked to Connie, about my desire to buy a home, he had offered his beach house in Malibu as a place I could stay in the interim. He was almost never in Los Angeles, especially now that I was handling his business.

My brother and I had packed our belongings and headed twenty miles up the coast. The home that Connie owned was on stilts and jutted out over the water. When there were storms the waves made the entire house shake. Liberace had originally owned it and literally every inch of the interior was mirrored. Even the doors were mirrored. The effect was quite stunning but, until one got used to it, very disorienting.

The day we moved in, Richard and I took our bedrooms and began exploring. He called me into his room and I entered to find him holding a remote control. He could not figure out what it was for. No matter how many times he pushed it, nothing happened. Suddenly, the front door of the house burst open and half a dozen fully armored men, in armored vests and head shields, poured in, with machine guns ready.

The button Richard was pushing, activated an alarm that was monitored by an elite security company that catered to the rich and famous. I was at the top of the stairs when they burst in. Instead of feeling fear and cowering in their presence, which would have been the normal reaction they were used to, I found the situation hilarious and, much to their consternation, burst out laughing. The men downstairs however, were not amused, and pointed their guns right at me.

At gunpoint they made us identify ourselves and explain why we were in Cornelius Santos' home. They remained grim faced as they made it clear we were never to touch the alarm remote unless our lives were truly in danger. We agreed and they departed. On the way out I know that I saw one of the men start laughing, he too, was overtaken by the absurdity of the situation.

Working with Connie was a unique experience. We did everything first class. When Connie was out of town, which was almost all the time, I had full use of his stretch limo and driver. When he was in the country, every day was a new adventure. One time we flew to New York City, where we met with Rick Hilton. Connie wanted to open high-end casinos in Peru and he wanted Hilton to do the hotels.

He asked me to invite Andrea, so I called her up and soon thereafter the three of us descended upon the Big Apple for a day of meetings and a week of fun. We dined at Tavern on the Green and drank at The 21 Club. Andrea was still a bit peeved with me, but she was not about to pass up a free week of fun in New York. We ended up having a blast.

Back in Malibu, I decided to have a party. I invited all my friends from the Marina as well as new business contacts. My brother invited but two people. One was a new girlfriend he'd met, while shooting an episode of the "Love Boat"; the other was a movie producer named John Daly.

56

JOHN DALY

John Daly was an engaging, intelligent and good-looking man who had just produced the first in a string of hits that would mark him as one of the most powerful producers in Hollywood. His resume would go on to include films such as "The Terminator", "Platoon" and "The Last Emperor".

He caught my attention right away. He looked like the sweetest man in the world, but I would soon learn that this was not a man to be trifled with. I got a feeling in my stomach, a physical reaction to his presence. We launched into conversation and soon thereafter we launched into a short lived but torrid relationship.

I became an accessory of his, at a number of celebrity events. We paraded through the crowd as John extracted information and proposals like he was harvesting a crop. His reputation within Hollywood was controversial. Years later, in November 1988, a front page article, in LA Business, would run with the headline; "JOHN DALY, DEVIL INCARNATE?" John had learned his tricks of the trade, as a boxing promoter, working with the infamous Don King.

I got a close enough look to know that I was no fan of the way John dealt with people. The wheeling and dealing did not sit well with my British sense of decorum. Still, the man had startling blue eyes and charisma that you could not deny. For a few months we were as hot as can be, then things cooled and I knew John Daly was not the man for me.

John Daly was, however, the man that got me pregnant.

57

MY OH MY, I'M PREGNANT

I was 38 years old, I was single, I had a sister born with Down's Syndrome, my business needed my full attention, and my doctors told me I should abort the pregnancy. However, there was never a doubt in my mind that I was going to have my baby.

Perhaps Karolina's death had opened the way for a new soul to come into our family. Out of the fourteen children in her family, Karolina was the only one who had lived to have children of her own. My child would start a new generation, one born into the light, not the darkness I had known. Besides, my business was thriving, I was about to close escrow on a beautiful home, and I was in great physical shape.

Though my getting pregnant was a total accident, I could not deny that I'd been getting feelings that I was missing something in my life. As soon as I became pregnant, I knew that what I was missing, was a child. I had no desire for two children; however, I would do this without John Daly. After two miserable failures in the husband department, I had no intention of marrying a man like John, not to say that he had any thought of asking. I was more than capable of taking care of myself and I was confident I could also take care of a baby.

By the time I knew I was pregnant, John and I had already broken up. I had no intention of telling him about my pregnancy but Richard was insistent that John had a right to know. In hindsight, I wish my brother had kept his advice to himself. However, at the time I called John and asked to see him.

As I have stated before and as I will state again, I hate confrontation but when it is necessary, I don't back away. I went to see John and I told him that I was pregnant, that I was going to have the baby, and I did not expect anything from him. The child was my responsibility. John surprised me. He said he wanted to help support me with the child. He was not an angry, scared jerk; he was supportive and strong. For that I give him kudos. If he had been telling the truth, I would give him even more.

58

A SHOCKING OCCURRENCE
(1982)

In the end John's assistance peaked with the nursery he helped my brother set up in my new house. After that he was almost nonexistent in the lives of either me or my child, reaching out every now and then, to spend a few fleeting moments with his son. I was on my own and I preferred it that way. I know that while, it is wonderful for a child to have a good father, I also know how damaging it can be for a child to have a bad father. Eight years later, John would do something that would leave no doubt in my mind that he would have been a bad father for my child.

As soon as I knew I was pregnant I began preparing for my baby's arrival. I negotiated the right to move into the house I was buying, right away, before escrow even closed. The last thing I wanted to be doing was move into a new home just prior to giving birth. My brother moved to the Palisades with me and helped me begin baby-proofing my new home.

The day I moved in, I felt as if all was right with the world. My new home was incredible. The grounds were lovely and as I said before, the neighborhood was top notch. Over the first couple months of being there, I saw Jane Fonda a couple more times. This was right when she was the queen of aerobics and at the forefront of a national fitness craze.

I had been doing my exercise regimen on a daily basis for close to a year, by that time, and her proximity only heightened my commitment to my program. In fact, prior to moving in, I had attended some classes at a gym she owned, on the west side. As a result of my program, I was in the best physical shape of my life as I progressed through my pregnancy.

Though I had only been working with Connie Santos for about a year, he had become a very important person in my life. He was always exhilarating to talk too and his business IQ was extremely high. In the preceding months we had sold hundreds of thousands of pounds of shrimp and we had more orders than we could fill.

There was no doubt that Connie would have loved to expand our relationship beyond the business realm, but as he was married, that was not a possibility. Once Connie understood this, he transferred his desire for me into affection. From the moment Connie had learned that I was pregnant, he'd become very protective. It was quite cute, actually.

About five months into the pregnancy, I felt like I was ready to have my child and that work would not be a problem. I was already looking for people to hire, who could help handle part of the load. Connie and I had been working on plans to establish our own farms and a quick-freezing plant, in Peru. We were on the verge of becoming big players in the shrimp business.

One day, I called him to discuss these plans and also to check on a large order that was running a couple days late. Connie got on the phone and as I started speaking to him I could sense that something was wrong. However, Connie assured me that everything was fine. The shrimp would arrive by plane the next day.

However, the next day came and no shipment was delivered. It was the same story the day after that, and the day after that. Finally, I got Connie back on the phone and I told him to tell me the truth. "What was happening?" There was a deep breath on the other end and then Connie told me.

The first thing he told me was that the order wasn't coming; he was strapped for cash and in danger of watching his entire empire collapse. New energy policies instituted by the United States had thrown the spot oil market into turmoil. Connie had been caught with orders he could not afford to fulfill. For the last few months he'd been burning through every asset he owned. He'd hoped that things would turn around, but they hadn't.

Over the past few weeks, he'd been forced to pull every penny out of the shrimp business, and every other business he had a part of. We were going out of business. I sat back absolutely stunned. I had just gone from being a woman with a golden future to an about-to-be broke single mom. Connie wasn't finished though; he had more to tell me.

Connie, a lifetime smoker, was in the last stages of cancer of the larynx. He had known for months, but had not wanted to worry me. Connie wouldn't live to see my new child and our business together wouldn't live to see the next day.

Connie excused himself and got off the phone. I told him goodbye and just sat there stunned. The man who had endless amounts of money, who vacationed on yachts, who flew on private jets in an era when this was almost unheard of, and finally the man that I had come to cherish, was dying.

Due to the danger in Peru, and the advanced state of my pregnancy, it was impossible for me to even think of flying down and putting the deals together myself. I was out of business, that was it. I would get calls for months from distributors begging me for shrimp, but there was nothing I could do.

It was a stunning blow to lose Santos from my life at this key moment. It changed my fate dramatically. I felt like my legs had been cut out from under me. As an expectant mother my options were greatly reduced. I had no one to look to for help; except myself. If I hadn't been pregnant, I could have done a thousand things. But now I had to figure out how to survive this terrible blow. There was a child, growing inside of me.

59

AN ALL AMERICAN BOY

It was not lost upon me that while I was nurturing a child inside me, I was watching the rebirth of Poland on TV. I thought to myself that if only my mother could have lived a little longer. The thought of having a grandson on the way and the chance that her Polish people could regain their freedom, may have given her the will to live on. Such thoughts made me melancholy for the mother I had only had fleeting moments with. I would wipe my eyes and vow to be the mother to my son that I never had.

The first cracks in the Iron Curtain were showing, and they were being banged open by the Poles. In 1979, a ship worker named Lech Walesa, led a movement, which resulted in the first non-communist labor union in a Warsaw Pact nation. Having been raised by a Polish labor organizer, I was enthralled with what was happening.

In 1981, the entire country of Poland had caught fire with the concept of revolution. By the end of the year, the Solidarity union and movement was made illegal. Most of the leaders, including Lech Walesa, were jailed. However, in 1982, unlike earlier uprisings in Poland, Hungary and Czechoslovakia, which had been crushed, the Solidarity movement would not die.

The collapse of my business with Connie was causing trauma in almost all aspects of my life. I fixed my attention on my housing dilemma. I was buying a house I could no longer afford. I proactively approached the sellers and renegotiated an extension with the money in escrow being used as rent. I would be able to stay in the house for three months after my child's birth.

Even though I was taking it in the shorts on the money in escrow, I still had some cash on hand. Between the sale of my flat in London and a $12,000 reimbursement from the IRS, I had enough money to cover me for a few months.

At the same time, I got an unexpected proposal from Wheeler. Our divorce had continued to grind on and I decided it was time to get it over with. He had ultimately succeeded in getting the jurisdiction changed to South Carolina and our attorney, in Pennsylvania, had told me point blank that it could be ten years before I could get a judgment against Wheeler.

Wheeler had the means and the know-how to keep his assets out of my hands for years, if not forever. I also knew that Wheeler had moved a lot of money offshore into accounts that the government would never find. I made the decision that it was time to settle. It also was important for my psyche to get it over with, before my child was born.

Five years after we split apart, we came to an agreement. Wheeler would pay my $75,000 legal bill and I would forsake any rights to his assets. I gave away millions, but I did not want any of his energy in my life. If I had not settled, I might still be at war with him.

As an aside, out of the blue, I got another legal document in 1982. My first husband, Wlodek, had actually been pushing an annulment through the Roman Catholic Church for years. Finally, just before my son's birth, that too came through. I was completely free of the two men I had been connected to for so many years.

On Independence Day, July 4, 1982, I gave birth to Jonathan Richard Daly. John Daly insisted that the baby bear his name. In light of the fact he said he wanted to be part of his son's life, I agreed. I did however change the spelling and made his first name Jonathan. John Daly always resented the fact I'd changed it, but my son would have his own identity. His middle name is in honor of my brother.

Jonathan and I went home and for the next month, I began the wonderful relationship with my son that I am blessed to have to this day. In all honesty, my son truly taught me how to love someone. For the next eighteen years we would live together as a team. There would be times he suffered for decisions I made and others times that I wanted to throttle him, but all in all, we survived and ultimately thrived.

I vowed that Jonathan would always know that his mother loved him. There would be no stony silences in our household, nor would yelling be common currency. He would know what it was to be hugged and loved by a parent. I had two incredible anti-role models in the parenting department. Whenever I wasn't sure what to do for my son, I could ask myself what my parents would do and then do the exact opposite. My son is by far my greatest achievement and I am proud to have him as my legacy.

Three months after Jonathan was born, we moved into a small house in Beverly Hills. While I recuperated and nurtured my son, I watched the reports of new rioting in Poland as the country stood up to the communist regime. Solidarity shocked the world by surviving the summer and pledging to keep the revolution going. In Los Angeles, supportive Americans placed lit candles in their windows, warming my heart and further deepening my love for America and its people. I too, was going through a revolution, reinventing my life as a single mother, a single mother who needed a job fast.

60

SEVERIN
(1983)

It so happens that prior to meeting John Daly, I had gone out a couple times with a wealthy man named Severin Wunderman. We had met through mutual friends at a party. Severin owned a company called Severin Montres; and would soon acquire homes in London, Paris and Switzerland; a castle in Grasse, France; Penthouses in New York and L.A.; a small ski resort in Utah; and last but not least, a yacht. Severin also collected art, and ultimately he wanted to collect me.

Severin's company owned the right to make and distribute Gucci watches. He had created a category he called "Boutique Watches". He believed that he could convince people to buy multiple watches so they could match their watch to their outfits. It turns out he had been right and his business was booming.

A couple months after Jonathan was born, Severin called me. He already knew what had happened with my business and that I was looking for the right opportunity. He told me that his watches were selling so quickly that he needed help. I agreed on the spot to join his company. I had a live-in maid, who was wonderful with Jonathan, so I was able to start work immediately.

Severin had made a brilliant marketing move and arranged for American Express to include an offer for his Gucci watches in the monthly bills they sent out to their customers. The recipients responded and the watches were flying out of the warehouse. At that point, Severin had a small operation on Fairfax Avenue, in Los Angeles, and I had a lovely little commute.

I started out doing basic tasks and within a month Severin promoted me to the head of purchasing. Things were chaotic, inefficiencies abounded, and details were falling through the cracks. Just the kind of situation I thrive in. We were selling watches like there was no tomorrow. We ended up being the single most profitable license that Gucci had. My role increased until I was actually helping to design the new watches. The business skills I had honed over the years with Brian, and then at Buzzard's Point, were serving me well. Unfortunately, there was trouble brewing.

Severin and I had enjoyed a few light romantic encounters, when we first met, but I had no idea that he was now falling in love with me. This was most likely because I had my knickers in a twist over Duncan Barker, the man who had been part of our group in the Marina.

Duncan was a top international executive with First Interstate bank, who had come to America from England. We had not been involved before, though there had been an undeniable attraction between us. For some reason we both resisted and before we ever acted upon our feelings, he had been transferred to Argentina and seemingly out of my life.

In April 1982, however, Argentina took possession of the Falkland Islands. This triggered a conflict which forced Duncan, and the other British subjects, in Argentina, to leave the country. Six months after I started working with Severin, Duncan appeared back on the scene.

The first time I saw him was at a party, I had at a home I had taken in Bel Air. When we said "hello", I immediately sensed that the chemistry we'd resisted before was still there. I could see him circling and again my instincts told me to resist. I insisted a girl friend stay with me, until he left for the evening. A short while later, I held another party, yes, I had a lot of parties. I tried the same maneuver, but this time Duncan outlasted my girlfriend.

Once my shield was down, I was defenseless. Duncan could see the desire in my eyes, he grabbed me in a hard embrace and then I melted into his lips. We spent the night together and were soon inseparable. After a few months, he moved in with my son and me. For a short period of time I thought that we would end up getting married. As weeks went by though, it became clear that Duncan was not cut out to be a father.

Duncan liked Jonathan, but he did not love him. Duncan was an only child and had been single his whole life. He just wasn't cut out to father a young son; especially one that wasn't his. It was very painful and it broke my heart to break up with him. He was a special man.

Even after we stopped living together, we continued to see each other at parties. Whenever we did, we would inevitably wind up together for the night. There was no denying the passion, but it just wasn't meant to be. Jonathan was my first priority and that was that.

With all this in the background, I can see why I was blind to Severin's growing infatuation with me. I would later find out, from Severin's maid, that he had become completely obsessed with me. She told me that he had photos of me up all over his house. I thought Severin was a friendly business confidant who was taking over the mentor role that Brian Kent had played for so long. Instead he was a man dreaming of a much larger relationship than the one I was enjoying.

Before I knew the depths of Severin's feelings, I proposed a major shift in the way the company handled distribution. After analyzing the business, it was clear that our distribution center should be moved from Los Angeles to Switzerland, where the watches were manufactured. If we did this, the profit margin on each watch would increase substantially.

I proposed this idea to Severin and he agreed. He put me in charge of the project, much to the consternation of the company's president. Severin went on to tell me that once the new system was in place, I would take over as president, in Switzerland. If the existing president had been upset before, he was foaming mad now. His entire future with the company was threatened. Unbeknownst to me at the time, he soon launched an all out campaign to destroy me.

61

THE UNWANTED PROPOSAL
(1984)

A short while later, Severin asked me to come to his house for a business meeting after work. I thought it was odd that he'd want to meet at his house, but as the sun was setting for the day, I drove to his house. Once there, Severin proceeded to propose to me. He told me that all he had could be mine: the homes; the yacht; the ski resort; all of it. He was offering me a life of utter luxury. He wanted me to marry him and his manner made it obvious that he assumed I wanted to marry him.

I was shocked by his proposal and before thinking, I told him the truth. I did love Severin, but not romantically. Severin was shocked. It had not entered his mind that I might turn him down. He fumbled for something to say as I sat there awkwardly. I stood up, gave him a kiss on the cheek and left.

I drove to a restaurant where I met Duncan. By the time I got home, that night, my answering machine was completely full. I hit play and I heard the first of a series of long rambling messages from Severin. Each was more painful to listen to than the one before it. By the time my machine had cut him off for good, he was sobbing into the phone and begging me to reconsider.

As one would imagine, work was incredibly awkward. Luckily, it was soon time for me to head to Switzerland. An assistant was going with me, but as I had no idea how long I'd be staying, on this first trip, I made other arrangements for Jonathan. I decided that the best thing to do was to put Jonathan in the charge of a nanny and have them stay at my father's flat in England. My father agreed, swayed by my logic that he'd have the benefit of the nanny as well. Though my father was a horrific father, I knew he would spend his time reading and my son and the nanny would be left alone.

With Jonathan in London, I'd be able to see him every weekend. Just two weeks before we were set to leave, my father called to tell me that he didn't want Jonathan and some stranger staying with him. I didn't have time to dwell on my father's behavior; I had to make new arrangements for my son.

Jonathan adored the nanny I had in Los Angeles, so I asked Vivian if Jonathan could stay with her and her husband. Vivian agreed and, a few days later, I rented them a new apartment, and then took off for what would turn out to be a three-month stay, in Switzerland. My eyes teared up as the plane lifted off from the runway. I was mortified at the thought of being away from my little boy for so long. For the next three months I lived out of my suitcase, as I started to reorganize the Swiss operation.

A month into my stay, we put on a big party for all of our major vendors. Severin flew in, and upon seeing him, I could tell that he was still not over my rejection. After the party, Severin and I got in the elevator, to head up to our rooms. Before anyone else could get in, Severin put up his hand and told the people standing there to take the next elevator. The doors closed and as soon as the elevator started moving, he pushed the emergency stop button and we came to an abrupt stop between floors.

Severin turned, grabbed my wrists, and pinned me up against the wall. It happened so quickly I had no idea how to respond as Severin pushed his face close to mine. He looked into my eyes and with incredible intensity, uttered these exact words, "It's not over, yet!" I said nothing and after a moment, Severin seemed to realize that he had crossed the line. Suddenly subdued, he let go of me and quickly turned to start the elevator. I stood still, not wanting to do anything to worsen the moment.

From that moment, my days working for Severin became more and more stressful. The tension between Severin and I only magnified the great pangs of loneliness I felt as I reached out each night to hug the son that wasn't there. I threw myself into work with a vengeance.

The stress at work, and the heartache I felt from being away from my son, caused my lifelong battle with insomnia to resume. I lay in bed with my eyes open picturing my little boy. I had never missed anyone in my life the way I missed Jonathan. I moved from my hotel room to an apartment, but it did nothing to ease my pain.

Back in Los Angeles, where many of the world's best athletes were competing in the 1984 Olympics, Severin's president was looking for opportunities to stab me in the back. Severin, who had been my biggest defender, was now only too willing to believe the lies he was being fed.

The irony of it all was that I had told Severin, before I left, that there was something wrong with the way the president was acting. I told Severin I suspected that the man was having clandestine conversations with Gucci, in a move to get the license for himself. It would turn out that I was right about this. There were other things he was planning, though, that would surprise even me.

After three months, I returned to Los Angeles to a world filled with uncertainty and sabotage. Everything about the future was up in the air. It was unclear how long I would be in town before heading back to Switzerland to take over the presidency I'd been promised. I didn't have a home to stay in, having given it up prior to my trip.

While I had been away, the Los Angeles office had been moved sixty miles south, to Orange County, meaning I had to be in Irvine on a daily basis. I wasn't sure what to do. Jonathan was happy and comfortable with Vivian and her husband. He would be coming with me to Switzerland in a month, so it didn't seem logical to rent a new place and move into it, only to have to leave.

Severin had an apartment complex in Beverly Hills where he suggested I stay, until it was time to head back to Switzerland. I took him up on his offer, thinking, finally I could be reunited with my son. There was one problem; the apartment I was to stay in only had two bedrooms and I was not alone.

The room I was squatting in was filled with his daughter's clothes. The other, was occupied by one of his sons, who just happened to be heavily involved with drugs. Nefarious characters were around constantly and it was impossible for me to even think of having Jonathan set foot in such a place. Jonathan stayed with Vivian and her husband, while I started a daily four-hour commute.

By the time I'd fight my way home, at night, I'd race over to Vivian's house just in time to watch Jonathan drift off to sleep.

It was incredibly frustrating and things at work were just as bad. Shortly after my return, one of my assistants called out to me in the parking lot. As if he was out of central casting, he looked around to insure no one was watching, and proceeded to tell me that the current president had a plan to get me out of the company.

I found myself embroiled in corporate politics again. I plugged away in uncertainty and while I did so, I began to fray around the edges. I was constantly battling with foes, battling with traffic, arriving at Vivian's apartment a moment after my son had fallen asleep, and to top it off, I was sleeping in an apartment that I shared with a drug addict and his friends. I was getting exhausted and my body was shedding pounds I could ill afford to lose.

Severin, not able to overcome his humiliation, began to treat me with lightly veiled hostility. Finally, the president made his move and claimed that I had stolen a large shipment of our watches. The last shipment that had gone out from our Swiss offices, while I was there, had never turned up in our California warehouse. Severin would later tell me that the president himself and another employee had committed the crime, but at the time Severin used the accusation as an excuse for firing me.

In the end, after three years of dedicated work, and tremendous success, all I walked away with was a five thousand dollar severance check. Severin would come to me, a year later, and apologize for his boorish behavior, but by then of course, it was far too late to undo the damage.

Hurt, but in some ways relieved, I went directly from Severin's office to Jonathan. I hugged him as if there was no tomorrow. I felt like a fool for having turned my life upside down for a man who had, in the end, betrayed me because of his own sexual and romantic insecurities.

Once again, I had to pull myself up and remake myself. First though, I needed to be back with my son.

62

SURVIVING SEVERIN
(1985)

I was emotionally and physically drained. Eight years after leaving Wheeler I had been broken down again. The depression and insomnia that had plagued me since my childhood were always right below the surface, ready to pounce. The events of the preceding six months had brought them raging forth again. Like a tidal wave consuming the coast, I was powerless to stop them from overcoming my delicate psyche.

I had saved money over the preceding three years, so I moved Jonathan and I into a nice apartment in Beverly Hills. By the time the furniture was in place, and the utilities turned on, I was barely functioning. I felt like I needed to sleep for a year, yet even an hour was almost impossible for me to manage. Nightmares from my youth burst through my brain at the first sign of slumber. My weight continued to drop and my depression deepened.

A dark cloud descended upon me. Severin's betrayal, Santos' death, John Daly's total desertion, my father's ongoing psychosis and my mother's death; the accumulated wounds were just too much for me. They took turns tormenting me as I lay in bed, exhausted. My son is what kept me striving to find a way out of the maze I was trapped within.

In the mornings, years of habit and the knowledge that my son needed his mother healthy, helped me force myself up to do my exercise program. I'd put on a workout outfit and go through one of my exercise tapes. Every day it would be a different tape, causing me to be constantly exercising new groups of muscles.

Once I finished, I would sit at the table and do the studying necessary to get the real estate license I had set my sights on. Real Estate had always intrigued me and I knew I could not work for anyone else again. After Wheeler and Severin, I could never again trust someone else to hold my destiny in their hands.

As my money ran out, I began purging my closet and drawers of the jewelry and furs I'd accumulated over the years. One way or the other, I was going to make it. I had my child to take care of. My health was still poor, as was my mental state, but I had to do something. At that time, a friend of mine, Jolyon Wilde, suggested I think about getting my real estate license. I did think about it and soon decided it was a good idea.

63

READY FOR REAL ESTATE
(1986)

I knew that if I had my real estate license, I could replenish my coffers and set out in an industry where the sky was the limit. I have always been able to look at something and see the potential in it. There's a feeling I get in my gut when I see a good deal. My gut told me that this was the right time for me to get into real estate. No matter how down I felt, I got up every day and studied.

Daily chores were still a challenge as I readied myself to take the test. On more than one occasion, I would have to pull over, in my car, because I would suddenly have no idea where I was. It was as if my entire electrical system would shut off and I could not process the sounds and images cascading down upon my brain. Sometimes, I'd become reoriented in five minutes and sometimes I'd have to sit there for an hour.

About six months after leaving Severin, I took the real estate exam and gained my license. I decided to focus on commercial real estate as I saw more opportunity there. Plus, I was much more comfortable speaking with businessmen than housewives.

With my license in hand, I went to work for Jolyon's company. I was left to my own devices and I began marketing myself aggressively. My print ads quickly caught the attention of a top exec at Marcus Millichape, a prominent commercial real estate company. They made a flattering offer, but I had no desire to hang my hat on somebody else's hook, especially after Jolyon had been so kind, besides, I knew I'd be going out on my own soon. After a year I thanked Jolyon for his help and did so.

Just over two months from the day I earned my license, I made my first sale, and received a commission check for $30,000. It was from a deal I did with a man named Johann Lippert, who would be a very important and valued client for me, over the next few years.

I was still not 100 percent better. I had to focus all of the energy I could on my new business. I was out of the house much of the day and I could see that it was hard on Jonathan. Even though he loved his nanny, he missed his mother. I put all my focus on Jonathan, my business and my health. I had neither the time nor the energy for men. My exercise regimen helped my body recover and with each new deal, my depression was pushed back beneath the surface a bit further. I was once again becoming Basia.

In the course of my work, I found an apartment complex that was undervalued. I had one of my gut feelings: this building could be turned for a nice profit; if I could move on it quickly enough. There were two problems: I needed more money than I had and my credit was still decimated from losing my home in the Palisades.

When I had done my first real estate deal with Johann, he had told me that I may look lovely (his words, not mine) but when it came to business, I thought like a man and he liked that. I decided to call him up and see if he'd like to jump into this deal. We went to the apartment building and I walked him through my refurbishing plans and my sales projections. By the end of the day, he had agreed to loan me the money I needed for the down payment. He bought it in his name and then quit claimed the building over to me. From the moment the building was in my name I was consumed with fixing it up.

For the next two months, I had crews repainting, spackling, changing drapes, planting flowers, sodding the lawn and cosmetically giving the entire building a make over. I put in security gates and in general, made it a much nicer place to live. By the time I was done, it looked like a new building. I put it back on the market and was immediately hit with offers, but none of them were high enough for my taste.

Pushy agents pressured me to take their client's offers, but I held out. After four months, I found the price I was looking for. Upon closing escrow, I was able to pay back Johann and pocket the balance. I was back.

64

LA COSTA
(1987)

My appetite was whetted now. There was no question about it; I was back and I was hitting my stride. Near the end of the year, I came across an opportunity that screamed out to me. There were six homes for sale in La Costa, a resort horse and tennis community, north of San Diego. A movie producer owned them all, and was desperate to sell them so he could finance a new project.

He was offering the six homes at a price, well below market value. I negotiated a deal with his realtor and then went to work, finding an investor to split the down payment with me. Though I had only spoken to him sporadically over the years, I called John Daly and offered the deal to him. After all, it was a win-win for John. He would make money and the mother of his son would make money. Surprisingly, John said he would do it and that his attorneys would handle everything, since he would be out of the country for a few months.

Pleasantly surprised, I proceeded to do the deal. It was a rather complicated transaction that involved the sale of my apartment building. Just three days prior to the scheduled closing, and after numerous unreturned phone calls, John's attorney sent me the contract via fax. As I was reading through it, I realized they were trying to pull a fast one on me. Not only did he want half of the profit for putting up half the money, he also wanted an egregious amount of interest on the money he was putting up. They obviously assumed that, even if I read the agreement, it would be too late for me to do anything but accept the new terms they'd added.

I was incensed. I called John immediately, but was unable to get hold of him. After a day of calls it was obvious he was avoiding me. I was so furious over his underhanded techniques that I immediately started thinking of where I could get the rest of the money, without him. If I didn't close it, I wouldn't just lose out on the opportunity; I would also find myself liable for taxes on the money I had made by selling the apartment building.

The very next day, I got a call from Johann Lippert. He wanted me to negotiate the purchase of another apartment building he'd had his eyes on. He asked me what I was working on and I told him about the deal that John Daly had just messed up. Johann told me that based on our track record, he'd loan the other half of the money to me. The deal ended up working out perfectly.

As I knew I would, I got a call from John a few days later, innocently asking me how the deal was going. I answered that he couldn't be so naïve as to think I was going to accept his new terms. The deal was done and he was out. John said he was shocked and swore he had no idea what his attorney had done, and that he should be the one in the deal. I just laughed and told him that I knew he was lying and he was too late.

I was able to rent out all six houses and refinance them in such a way that Johann was paid back and I ended up with all six homes under my name. I had a nest egg; one that I would need in the years to come.

65

LANDING IN LA JOLLA

Prior to the La Costa deal, I had gone to a Club Med in Ixtapa, Mexico, with Jonathan. It was a wonderful facility that catered to families. The trip was a reward for the tough time we had come through. At the darkest of moments, my little boy had been there to give me a hug and words of encouragement. When we arrived at the resort, I met a woman who would become a wonderful friend of mine. Her name was Phyllis Kaiser.

Phyllis had a son, Arthur, who was the same age as Jonathan. Though Phyllis' profession was that of a teacher, she'd just inherited a good deal of money and was getting involved with real estate. We hit it off immediately and before the week was out, she suggested that Jonathan and I move to La Jolla and live with her and her son.

After we returned from Ixtapa, Jonathan and I drove down to check out the area. We both loved it. Jonathan and Arthur bonded immediately, and instinctively I knew that Phyllis and I would go on to be lifelong friends.

Truth be told, I was tired of Los Angeles. I did enjoy parts of it, for example, I'd recently started dating a man named George Milton. He looked like Charlton Heston and was a member of the Film Academy. On his arm, I would attend events such as the Oscars, Emmys and Golden Globes. But all in all, the city reminded me of the tragic demise of Connie and the horrid betrayal of Severin.

Jonathan and I moved down to La Jolla, in 1987, after Phyllis and I had found a large, beautiful ocean view home to lease. The four of us created our own unique family. We hired a maid, to make sure that the boys were never alone, and soon thereafter added our maid's sister to our payroll. Phyllis and I had a lot of fun. Business was good and the environment we lived in was fantastic. The downside was that I still had properties to watch over in Los Angeles and I was gone quite a bit.

After I had negotiated the apartment deal for Johann, he had asked me to manage that building and several others with a total of 350 apartments. They were spread out, all over Southern California. I was on the road, all the time. I would literally have to knock on the doors of these inner-city apartments to ask for any overdue rents. Contrary to what one might think, I never had any undue problems with the tenants.

Due to the experiences of my own life, I could empathize with people going through hard times. I also treated our tenants with the utmost respect. I have always tried to conduct myself in a humble and honorable manner, both in business and in my personal life. Perhaps the people there treated me kindly because of that.

I was doing extraordinarily well: between Johann; my homes in La Costa and my other real estate ventures. The only problem was that I was driving hundreds of miles a week and I had to leave Jonathan in the care of our maids, far more than I desired.

One day, when I was knocking on apartment doors, two-and-a-half hours from home, I called in to check on Jonathan. There was no answer, which surprised me. I called again and again. Finally, a man, a policeman, answered the phone. My heart stopped for a moment, as immediately I asked if Jonathan was all right.

It turned out that some friends of Jonathan's and Arthur's had come over and they had started making prank phone calls. Unfortunately, some of them were to 911. When the police arrived they discovered that the calls were phony. Kids will be kids and they'd scared the boys badly enough that they wouldn't have to worry about more prank calls. What they were worried about, though, was the fact that a group of young kids were home alone with no supervision.

I was dumbfounded when he told me the boys were alone. I told him he had to be mistaken, we always had at least one adult housekeeper there, even when Phyllis and I were both home. The police questioned the boys further and they soon discovered our maid hiding in the closet. It turned out that her papers had expired and she was scared to death that she would be deported.

The police took pity on her and did not take her away. After a final warning to the boys, they left. Things were fine, but I was left unsettled by what had happened. The boys that had come over and instigated the prank calls were a little older than Jonathan. They seemed to be headed down the wrong path and I did not want my son following them.

It was impossible for me to be home as much as I would have liked and I could see that my son needed more discipline in his life. As much as it pained me to do so, I decided to put Jonathan into the nearest boarding school, which ironically, was run by nuns. Unlike when I had gone away, I discussed the idea with Jonathan. We went together to look at the campus. We both liked it. In fact, Jonathan was anxious to go, once he'd visited it.

It was a military boarding school and the students there wore the cutest little uniforms you've ever seen. It was close by, so I could see Jonathan on a regular basis. He came home for almost every weekend. Even so, in the second semester, Jonathan told me he wasn't happy there and that in fact he hated it. At the end of the term, I brought him home and our experiment with boarding school was over. Though, I did keep his little uniform.

66

BAD DAD
(1989 - 90)

Socially, I was still going to big Hollywood events. George Milton would take me to parties, where stars such as Jack Nicholson and John Ritter were likely to show up. Aside from the constant driving and time away from home, I felt like I had our lives on a smooth track. Life was fun.

Phyllis was quite attractive and had a busy social calendar of her own. We would play a game with the men that came to call on us. The first time a man came to pick one of us up, he had to meet with the other one in the foyer, where we'd interview them. One man took it so seriously; he actually brought his resume along.

Phyllis and I began discussing buying the La Jolla house together. Johann had proven to be a wonderful client and overall, business was good. I was looking forward to buying the home we were living in, with Phyllis, and giving Jonathan a stable home environment, where he could grow up with the same kids for years to come. Our little makeshift family was good for all of us.

Just as we were about to put the money into escrow Phyllis met a man that made her change her plans, drastically. This man gave me great cause for concern from the first time I met him. He was involved in banking and presented himself as a real estate entrepreneur. However, the deals he talked about just didn't seem to be the sure fire winners Phyllis thought them to be.

Things moved like lightning from the moment Phyllis met him. Our purchase was put on hold as he convinced her to put her money into two homes he wanted to buy, refurbish and sell. Shortly thereafter, they became engaged and Phyllis moved in with him. The day she and Arthur left was a sad day.

Our hybrid family was torn in half. I tried to finish the purchase myself but with the six homes from La Costa just starting to pay for themselves, I couldn't quite afford the down payment. Instead, Jonathan and I moved to a lovely little place near my homes in La Costa.

Phyllis never married her new partner and ultimately lost much of what she'd invested with him. I was sad that the plans Phyllis and I had made came to naught. However, it would turn out not to be the last time we lived together.

For the next two years I continued working with Johann and doing my own deals. My six homes were rented out and times were quite good. Then, in 1990, I got a call from Phyllis. She needed help with the homes she'd been stuck with, after breaking up with her fiancé. She asked if I would move back in with her. Jonathan and I both missed our days in the big old house in La Jolla. In many ways, Phyllis and Art were family. I decided to take her up on her suggestion.

I packed up our things and we moved to Fairbanks, an exclusive, gated section of Rancho Santa Fe, one of the most beautiful and expensive communities in America. The lots there are a minimum of five acres in size and the entire city is built within a beautiful Eucalyptus forest.

The Santa Fe railroad company had planted the trees years earlier. They were going to cut them down and turn them into railroad ties. However, it turned out that the wood of the Eucalyptus was too brittle and would break apart. Thus, the railroad sold the land to a developer who subdivided it and turned it into an incredible place to live.

Phyllis wanted me to pay her quite a bit of rent, to stay with her. I agreed but after the first month it was clear that she needed a lot of my time and energy so we had a quick renegotiation. The problem Phyllis had was that her home suffered from bad curb appeal and a horrible layout. We went to work and did everything we could to make it look better. Unfortunately, there was nothing we could do about the layout.

Though we had our family back together, John Daly's absence in Jonathan's life was quite conspicuous. As angry and disgusted as I was with John, I never tried to do anything to poison him in the eyes of his son. However, one day that all changed. When Jonathan was eight, he wanted to know his father. I called John and arranged for the two of them to have lunch together at the Beverly Center shopping mall. I drove Jonathan up, handed him over to John and left them alone. I trusted that John would be kind to his son. I should have known better.

When I came back to pick Jonathan up, after their lunch, I could tell immediately that something was wrong. We got in the car and, during the course of the two and a half hour drive home; I learned why Jonathan was distraught. During lunch, Jonathan had innocently asked his father why he never got to see him. John Daly had told him that the reason was that he didn't think that Jonathan was really his son.

Jonathan started crying as he told me. I could not believe what I was hearing. First of all, I knew that the only person it could possibly be was John. Second, John had never voiced his suspicions to me. Finally, what adult would do such a thing to a child? Jonathan was devastated and I was angry in a manner that only a mother can be. I wanted to turn around and rip the man's head off of his body. Instead we kept driving.

Jonathan would not see his father again until he was out of high school. They would have one more disappointing lunch and that would be, for all practical purposes, the end of their relationship. I have always been saddened by the fact Jonathan was raised without a real father. However, I know he would have been much worse off if John Daly had been his male role model. Luckily, two good men would ultimately enter Jonathan's life and provide the male guidance he needed.

67

GOOD DAD
(1991)

Around this time, I received the balance of a commission from a deal I'd negotiated for Johann, a few years earlier. I took the money and bought the flat my parents had lived in together, and which my father still occupied. I paid cash for it and gave the keys to my father. In perhaps my last attempt to connect to the man, I insured that he would have a nice and safe place to live for the rest of his life. If I had known what was coming I would have held onto the money.

Soon after moving to Rancho Santa Fe, I met a doctor named Kunzman, who was so pleased with my negotiating and business skills that he had me take over the management of all his properties. At first it seemed like he was going to be a new Johann. Unfortunately, I sorely misjudged this man, he was no Johann.

We started adding to his portfolio but somehow my commissions weren't keeping pace with his acquisitions. For almost a year, Dr Kunzman monopolized the majority of my time, but he consistently shorted me when it came time to settle up. Of all the people I've dealt with in my life, he was one of the worst.

Once I realized he was never going to pay me what he owed me, I told Dr Kunzman he was a user and a taker, though perhaps in slightly saltier language. As I told him what I thought of him, he stood there with his eyes staring at the ground. After letting him have it with both barrels, I walked away. The only good thing I had received from my time with Kunzman was an introduction to a remarkable man named Dan Burakowski.

Dan was a strong, friendly man who worked with his hands and lived the values he preached. He specialized in constructing beautiful staircases and ornate gates for estates. I met Dan through the course of his work and took an instant liking to him. Though we dated a few times, Dan and I were not meant to be. However, during our time together he had developed a true interest in Jonathan. Even after we stopped going out together, Dan would come by and take Jonathan out to play catch or to go to a movie. In effect, he became Jonathan's surrogate father.

He could tell that Jonathan was a good kid and something just clicked between the two of them. Dan was the one who taught Jonathan how to throw a baseball and shoot a basketball. He was the one that would take my son for walks and just talk about life from a man's perspective. Dan was a wonderful man and I often lamented the fact that I did not have romantic feelings for him.

Jonathan was so intent on bringing us together that he would give Dan detailed instructions on how to woo my heart. He told Dan which restaurant to take me to (Mille Fleur) and what type of flowers to hand to me when I opened the door (a dozen red roses). Dan followed Jonathan's instructions precisely, but to no avail. Dan would remain a wonderful influence on Jonathan through the years and will always hold a revered spot in my heart. I remain eternally grateful to him. He remains a good friend to both of us to this day.

When I wasn't helping Phyllis with her home, I was working on my other deals. Johann had lost his biggest apartment building, and to conserve cash, he took over the duties I was handling. It was a big ding in my income.

The economy had been slowing and a couple of my homes were unoccupied. As much as we enjoyed living with Phyllis, it made no sense for me to pay rent when I owned a lovely home that was sitting empty. Jonathan and I packed our things and parted ways again with Phyllis and Arthur.

One morning, soon after we moved back to La Costa, I woke up with a strange sensation in my arms. Over the next few days the sensation spread and within a week I was on my back in bed, with an infection that had overrun my entire system. Out of the blue, with everything going well, my body broke down and soon my mental state would do the same. I had climbed up out of the valley again, only to tumble into a new abyss; darker and deeper than those I'd fallen into before.

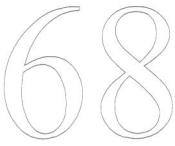

DEPRESSION
(1992)

Twice before I had broken down. In each case I had suffered horribly, physically and mentally. The first time had been after Don Wheeler's theft of all that I'd worked for over a five-year span. The second time had been after Severin fired me over a pack of lies and reneged on promises I was counting upon.

In both cases, I'd been betrayed and put through stressful trials and tribulations that had weakened me until I could no longer stand. This time my life was going wonderfully. When I first felt physically ill, I had a thriving real estate business and I owned six homes. My son was a bright young lad and the future looked positive on all fronts.

I was no stranger to illness, as I said, having suffered physically from my first days in Jerusalem. It was as if every attack I had ever suffered had retreated deep within my system, until suddenly, they had joined forces in a massive assault on my mental and physical capacities. I was like the Polish cavalry in the face of the Nazi stormtroopers – I was overrun.

Though the doctors could give me no diagnosis as to what was causing the infection that raced through my body, I knew what was coming. Sleep became an elusive concept more than a nightly visitor. When I did close my eyes, I awoke with nightmares racing through my head. Finally, a dark cloud descended and I felt the uncaring bonds of depression close around me.

The doctors course of action was to put me on one type of antibiotic after the other. The only thing they seemed to do was to further weaken my defenses. The weaker my body became, the more I started to worry about our finances. The more I worried about our finances, the more depressed I became. The more depressed I became, the weaker I got. I was caught in a vicious cycle that seemed to have no end.

Anyone who has truly suffered from depression can tell you that it is worse than most physical illnesses. It drains the hope from your soul and makes every movement an exercise in futility. The thought of getting out of bed weighs one down until movement is impossible and seemingly pointless. Doctors and friends wanted to shrug my depression off; as if it were something I was allowing myself to indulge in. Today, we understand much more about depression than we did in the early 90's. Depression is not something to be ashamed of.

The reality was, that the shame and hatred that had been thrust upon me, by my father's acts, so long ago, had lingered inside, forming a toxic cocktail that needed no excuse to take over my system. There was no therapy; there was no cure; I was left to my own devices to try and fight off a disease that had gone untreated for decades.

The worst thing for me was that my son was suffering because of my illness. I could see the fear in Jonathan's eyes as he watched his mother lie in bed, barely conscious. At times, I heard myself snapping at him in a voice that I didn't even recognize. One day I took Jonathan's hand and tried to explain to him that his mommy was not herself. There were tears in my eyes as I watched Jonathan try to understand an unfathomable situation.

69

ROCK BOTTOM
(1993)

At the same time my mind and body were crashing, the real estate market in Southern California was collapsing. By the end of 1993 my homes in La Costa had lost much of their value. All but two stood empty and I was in one of the two occupied homes.

On top of this, because of my physical condition, it became very hard for me to drive and thus work. As had happened to me before, I would be driving in my own neighborhood and suddenly I'd become totally disoriented. I would pull over to the side of the road and sit there, until I would eventually remember where I was.

I became so weak that I couldn't even hold the phone. I put the other La Costa homes up for sale, but the market was so bad that I had no takers. As my physical condition worsened, and our bills piled up, I was forced to take low-ball offers on two of the houses. The bank would soon take the others. I was headed towards rock bottom. One night as I went to sleep, I knew that the next day had to be different or one of these nights would be my last.

The next morning, I woke in such a fog that I had literally lost the ability to add simple sums in my head. It was now or never. I struggled against the physical pain and the emotional turmoil and sat up in bed. I forced myself to put on a pair of sweatpants and slip one of my exercise tapes into the VCR.

Though I could barely move, I finished the entire tape. I did the same thing the next day and the day after that. I continued to follow my regimen of large amounts of water complemented by fruits, vegetables and a small amount of meat and fish.

Finally, even the one home I had a tenant in, stopped producing income. The single mom who lived there lost her job and I didn't have the heart to evict her. It didn't matter anyway, because soon after she stopped paying, the banks stepped in and foreclosed, kicking us both out. My inability to work and the depressed real estate market had placed me in deep debt.

Finally, I made the devastating decision to go bankrupt. As part of the process I had to file for welfare. This was a tremendously troubling time, as I had never seen myself as someone needing such a handout. When I had my interview with the caseworker he asked me who the father was. I told him I'd never married the man but I knew who he was.

After what John had done to Jonathan, a couple years earlier, I was happy to hear the caseworker say that they were bound by law to go after the father, for support. They contacted John and told him to come to San Diego for a DNA test. If the test was positive, he would have to start supporting his son. John ignored the test date and the one scheduled after that. The caseworker moved to enforce a subpoena only to discover that John was not under their jurisdiction.

It turns out that John had been going in and out of the country for years on temporary visas and there was no legal standing with which to force him to San Diego.

70

THE END OF ZYGMUNT

After the La Costa homes were repossessed, Jonathan and I moved to nearby Solana Beach. Things were so bad that I actually took on the care of Phyllis' mother, who was near the end of her life. She took a room in my home and I became her caregiver.

Jonathan and I were living without a safety net. The only real asset I retained was my father's flat, which had not been taken, because it generated no income and was in my father's name. We were barely scraping by, but at least we were together and we loved each other. Our challenges had caused conflicts but they had also helped us bond at a level that would never be broken. A day didn't go by that I didn't give my son a huge hug and tell him how much I loved him.

Though I despised what Zygmunt had done to my mother and me, I still found myself wanting to have some sort of connection with my father. I think that I just couldn't believe that all there was, was the bad. The hardest part was trying to reconcile my existence and values with the life of the man from whom I had come. If Zygmunt was a truly evil person, could I be that much different?

Well, the answer is YES!

I can state unequivocally, that it does not matter where or who you come from, you are what you make of yourself. No matter what cards we have been dealt, we get to play our own hand. It is our responsibility to do the best we can and be the best we can.

In January 1993, I received a call from my brother. Zygmunt was dying. Money was still extremely tight but our dear friend Dan gave me the money to fly over. I got there in time to sit at my father's bedside, as he was drawing his last breaths on this planet. I looked at him and was about to ask how he was feeling when he unloaded on me. He proceeded to tell me that I had failed him as a daughter and left him an impoverished old man. I had betrayed him. He wasn't even grateful for the home I had bought him.

I sat there for a moment, stunned. Even at the last possible moment, when he could have chosen to try and show some level of humanity to me, he had chosen to lash out. I stood up and walked out of his hospital room. Later that night Zygmunt drew his last breath and died.

Any last redemptive thought I had for my father was extinguished. He was a bitter and broken man, down to his last moments on the planet. As brilliant as he was and as patriotic as he was, his true measure is best taken by his elder daughter whom he betrayed before the very God he spent so much of his later years studying so intensely.

71

CLOSURE

A couple days later I watched his coffin go into the fire, as he was cremated. It was a sense of profound relief that he was finally out of my life forever. As the flames devoured his physical remains I simply sighed. I stayed in London long enough to take care of Zygmunt's affairs. Our sister was already in a stable, state-supported, living environment, where she was doing well. My father's flat was transferred to my name and I drove over to inspect it. It had been a while since I had been inside of it, and I was shocked.

The ceilings were literally brown, from all the smoke Zygmunt's cigarettes had emitted over the years. Every inch of the flat was filled with books. They were in numerous languages and dealt with theology, history and philosophy. If they had been in vintage shape, his collection would have been instantly accepted, with thanks, by any major library in the world. However, every page, of every book, had his notes scribbled in the margins. In the end, the books were destroyed, as I did not have the funds to ship or store them.

As I went through the apartment, I reflected on the incredible intelligence that my father had possessed. I found myself wishing he had not done the horrible things he had, so that his brilliance could be celebrated. He had risked his life, fighting for his country. He had forsaken personal fortune, to fight for the rights of others. He had become a college professor, teaching courses on history and philosophy. However, as a victim of the dark side of my father's soul, I was left to lament the private life he lived and savor the fact that he was at last, out of mine.

I ended up renting the flat to my friend Frances' ex-husband who needed a place in the city to stay. I gave it to him at half the going rate in exchange for his promise to fix it up. I still own the flat, though I have long since gone in and done a very stylish refurbishing of it. Upon my return home, I felt as if the last dark cloud that had been raining down on me was gone. I was still quite weak, but somehow I knew that I was getting my life on the right track.

72

A DAY AT A TIME
(1994-95)

Upon returning from England, I was determined to wipe the last vestiges of my illness from my body and from my mind. I was more resolute than ever about following my exercise and nutritional regimen. I almost never missed a morning, in front of my VCR, doing one of the hundred or so workouts I had bought over the years.

The tapes were all from a company, called "The Firm", for whose products I still have the greatest affection. Their videos truly did help save my life and I remain a loyal customer to this day. In fact, if they ever want someone to put together a workout for those of us in our sixties, I'm their gal.

After the bouts I'd had with illness, I was very serious about my program. My son, and later, the love of my life, both came to call me the "Juice Nazi". I have to admit that quite often I'd simply yell out the word "Juice" and expect Jonathan to turn up a few minutes later with it. To be honest, it was the only chore I made him do, yet in his mind that was one too many, hence, Juice Nazi.

Jonathan and I were happy in Solana Beach. Phyllis and Arthur were nearby, as was Dan. Over the next two years Jonathan made a number of good friends as I continued to climb back up the mountain, a day at a time.

As I started to get back to work, we moved into a lovely home with six bedrooms and a sauna. It was gorgeous. Besides Jonathan and me, we leased it with a man named Waldo, and his son, along with a single woman named Pamela. Unfortunately, Pamela had the habit of forgetting to pay rent. Eventually, we had to ask her to leave.

My ongoing commitment to exercise and nutrition was irrevocable. I was determined to never again succumb to the type of illness that had almost killed me a few years earlier. Over the years, my program evolved until the point, that today, it is an essential part of who I am. You can find my daily workout and nutritional program in the addendum of this book.

73

THE RIGHT DON
(1996)

By 1996, I was getting back on my feet financially, and my health was nearly back to what it had been prior to my illness. I was a fifty-two year old single woman, with an outlook that was looking better and an ass that still looked great. I'm sorry ladies, but I couldn't resist. My son was a teenager who had some legitimate issues to act out about, but over all we had a good relationship. I continued to have a healthy interest in men, though I had no interest in getting married again.

I have always been comfortable on my own. My favorite times in childhood were when my father was gone and my mother left me alone to read. My favorite times at Buzzard's Point had been when Wheeler would go off on month long business trips and I would be alone with our dogs, my books and my classical music collection. I was content to live out my days as a single independent woman.

With things getting back on track in my life, I decided to have a party on Mother's Day. One of the couple's I had invited, David and Helen-Jo Thorpe, called me just a short while before people were supposed to arrive. They told me they could not come because a good friend of theirs had shown up at their door. I told them to bring him along and I hung up the phone.

About an hour later, I was standing near the kitchen when the front door opened and I saw a man standing there. Before he even stepped across the threshold I had a premonition, "I'm going to marry that man." He had a big grin on his face as he walked up and introduced himself. His name was Don Fuller.

I can say with confidence that marriage was not on Don's mind, as he walked over to introduce himself to me. He was in the middle of his third divorce and had just moved from Denver to Newport Beach. I welcomed Don into my home and we had immediate chemistry. This tall athletic looking man enthralled me. It was obvious that he was extremely intelligent and in his eyes, I could see a kindness that I would come to love.

During the course of the party, I found myself drawn to Don, again and again. The more we talked the more we realized how much we had in common. When he asked me for a cup of real English tea, I was only too happy to oblige. Each time we got to an interesting point in the conversation, however, the friends that had brought Don would shuffle him off to meet another woman at the party. They were under the misguided impression that Waldo was more than my roommate. They were hoping that Don would hit it off with a mutual friend named Linda. However, no matter how many times they pulled him away, Don came back.

Shortly after Don left with my friends, I got a call asking me if it would be all right to give him my phone number and address. I, of course instantly, said "yes". When your knickers are in a twist, there is no point in pretending otherwise.

Before we could get together, Don had to fly back to Colorado to take care of his divorce. I waited patiently to see if I would hear from this accomplished man again. One day I looked at my mail and found a letter from Colorado. He wanted to know if it would be all right to stop on his way back and meet me for lunch. From the way he worded things, I realized at that point that he too, thought I was involved with Waldo.

A week later, we met for the second time and over lunch I told him that I was in fact very single. With bright smiles on our faces we began to talk about our lives. It was soon apparent that we'd been playing a game of tag for decades.

Apart from the Tel Aviv harbor, and the day I had prevented him from swimming at the Skyline Hotel, it turned out he was also living in Pacific Palisades when I was pregnant and in La Jolla when I lived with Phyllis. Before the end of lunch, I knew that fate had finally put us together and he was meant to be mine.

After lunch we walked along the beach in Del Mar. The waves were shining as they broke along the shore. I felt Don take my hand in his and a moment later he drew me to him. I looked into his eyes and we paused for a moment. In an instant that felt like eternity we kissed and I pressed up against him. I felt like I was home. Whether he knew it or not, I was going to become Basia Fuller.

74

FALLING IN LOVE

After our lunch, Don and I were together as much as possible. He would drive down, from Newport Beach, to Solana Beach every chance he got. Even so, a three hour round trip was not conducive to a long-term relationship. Don and I fell in love so quickly that being apart was not an option. Even so, he was a perfect gentleman and kept our relationship on as cerebral a level as possible.

After two weeks, the passion we felt became overpowering. Finally, one night he took me into his arms and then into his bed. For once, my insomnia was welcomed, as we spent the night consummating a timeless love. From that moment on, I was his woman and he was my man.

I suggested that Don move in with me but he already owned two homes in Newport Beach and had new business concerns in the surrounding area. After moving so many times I was fully prepared to head up the coast. There was one significant problem, Jonathan did not want to go, he loved Solana Beach. Jonathan had a number of friends that were important to him.

Most importantly, he did not want to move away from Phyllis' son, Arthur, and his surrogate father, Dan.

I was conflicted, but I had a pragmatic reason for taking Jonathan out of Solana Beach. The following fall he was going to start high school. There were some older kids that Jonathan looked up to. Unfortunately, they were heavily involved with drugs. I could see trouble coming and I knew that if he was in a new school and community, his high school experience could be much safer.

Finally, I made a decision that was very hard, but in my heart I knew it was the right move for us. Three months after meeting Don, and in time for Jonathan to enroll for the start of high school, we moved to Newport Beach. Jonathan was very angry with me. After moving so many times, he felt that I was being selfish and that like men before him, Don would come and then he would go.

It was hard listening to his words and trying to explain that this was different. Inside I knew that Don was the man I'd always been searching for. His mind was brilliant and he'd honed his business skills over the years as the CEO of a computer company that had over five thousand employees. Don also understood real estate and owned a number of homes. Most of all I was deeply in love with him and he was deeply in love with me.

After we moved to Newport Beach, Jonathan and I experienced some hard times. I was strict with Jonathan and intent on keeping him on the straight and narrow. Jonathan was intent on proving to me that I had made a mistake. Meanwhile, Don did the perfect thing and stayed out of our battles. He seemed to understand what Jonathan was going through. He did not try and replace Dan as the man that Jonathan looked to for advice.

Don did not pretend that his relationship with me gave him any say over Jonathan. He respected Jonathan's right to fight with me and stayed out of our arguments.

Jonathan grew to ultimately respect and then love Don and eventually Jonathan grew to think of Don as his father. There were times I am sure he would have loved to trade me in for another mother, but he had no problems with Don. There was more than one time when I told him that I loved him with all my heart but at that moment, I sure did not like him.

While Jonathan and I were finding our equilibrium as mother and son, Don and I were learning about each other.

75

BECOMING A COUPLE
(1997)

Jonathan and I moved into one of Don's homes and Don was living in another. However, from the time we set foot in Newport Beach, he was in our house. Don and I were inseparable. It was as if our souls had been searching for each other for a lifetime. We were the lead characters in a love story that neither of us ever wanted to end. There were, however, obstacles to overcome.

Don thought like a CEO and approached our relationship from the standpoint that he was at the helm of the ship. I, on the other hand, had not been married since 1977, and no one was going to tell me what to do or where to go. I had been my own boss for years and we did butt heads numerous times. We both had to remember that there was another person in the relationship, whose feelings mattered as much as our own.

We worked through all these issues and throughout we were passionate in all aspects of our lives. We would love with abandon and then turn around and argue with each other over the boundaries we each needed in place. A moment later we would again be in each others arms.

After our five collective marriages, neither of us wanted to make a mistake again. One of the first things we did was to agree to keep our finances separate. I had my accounts and Don had his. This worked for both of us and helped keep our relationship on an equal level. As strong-minded as Don was, there wasn't a male chauvinistic bone in his body. He always listened and gave me the respect and space I needed.

76

EXCITING TIMES
(1998)

These were the most exciting and happy days of my life. After two mangled marriages, I was thrilled to experience a relationship based on love, passion and mutual respect. I didn't wake up looking for signs that things would fall apart, I woke up looking for that day's adventure.

Very shortly after we started our relationship, a friend of mine, from the old days in London, invited Don and me to a New Year's Eve extravaganza he was having on the estate he had bought in Poland. I was surprised when Don said he'd love to go. Six other friends flew in from London and we all stayed on the estate. Other faces from my past appeared, belonging to other refugees who had also returned to live in Poland. We partied for a week and Don enjoyed the festivities as much as I did.

We shared a love of traveling and embarked on numerous adventures. Over the years, Don and I would visit Brazil, Peru, Bolivia, China, Australia, New Zealand and... oh, you get the idea. On these trips, Don introduced me to the joy of jewelry. Up until this point in my life I had no real interest in rings, bracelets, necklaces and earrings. However, after a year with Don, I learned to appreciate the pleasure one could receive from pearls, diamonds, emeralds and sapphires. I was a quick learner.

When we weren't traveling, we were remodeling one of Don's homes. In total we redid four homes together. Don reveled in the opportunity to build things, being an engineer at heart. I had years of experience to draw upon and together we were quite a team. Don had bought a lovely home that we turned into a palace. When we sold it years later, we made a fortune on it. At the time, we were just having fun.

After we had been together for a couple years, we decided to take a trip to Europe with Jonathan and Don's two youngest children, Natalie and Greg. They had both spent time with us, and Jonathan and Greg were the same age. Before the trip they were acquaintances; after the trip they were siblings.

We bought a Plymouth Voyager specifically for the trip. We put it in a container that was shipped to England. Aside from the Voyager, we filled the container with tools, furniture and supplies; which we would subsequently use to remodel my flat. We proceeded to spend the summer driving throughout Europe.

I think we cemented our relationship in Berlin, where Don and I had the fight of our lives. I was navigating and he was driving. At one point I directed Don to turn left, which would have been suicide as there was no 'left'. Don proceeded to point out that my navigation skills sucked. I took umbrage at his tone and a moment later our tiff turned into a tsunami.

Ten minutes later, we calmed down, Don took over the navigation and I drove the rest of the way. We were soon laughing as if nothing had happened. I smiled, realizing that only a committed couple could have such a fight and carry on without worrying about any lasting damage. There was no turning back, we would be together forever. My heart fluttered and I think I gave the car a bit more gas.

Other than for our blow up in Berlin, the trip was a revelation for both of us, having both made trips on our own, years earlier. Right after World War II ended, fourteen year old Don Fuller had actually ridden his bike all the way from London to Warsaw, covering almost fifteen hundred miles in the process. He and a friend had cycled through the war torn continent as if they were on holiday. Their parents had no idea, thinking they were riding across England. Soldiers didn't pay any attention to the two young teenagers riding on roads that had been used by General Patton's tanks, less than a year earlier. The devastation Don had witnessed at that time had been beyond description.

Twenty years after Don's trip, I had set out on my aforementioned journey with Wlodek. At that time, I had refused to visit any concentration camps; on this trip we took the kids to as many as possible. We wanted them to understand what had happened in the peaceful lands we drove through. We wanted them to see the bullet holes, hear the stories and sense the suffering that so many had experienced just decades before.

When we entered Poland, I was struck by how aggressively the country was rebuilding itself. You would never know that this was the same devastated nation I had visited in 1965. Modern malls and offices were going up throughout the country. Cities were restoring lovely parks and creating pedestrian only blocks. The end result was that Poland was once again one of the jewels of Europe.

Over the course of our trip, the kids bonded. Don and I were thrilled to watch them become friends, and then something more. By the time we headed home, we were a family. Greg and

Jonathan would go on to consider each other brothers, and serve as Best Man at each other's wedding.

At the age of fifty-five, after a lifetime of searching, I had found my family, and with it, true happiness. Don and I had seen the best and worst of each other and our love had only grown. I had put my career on hold, but it had been well worth it. For the first time in my life, I was being loved unconditionally.

77

THIRD TIMES THE CHARM
(1999)

The next summer, we returned from another trip abroad to find that our neighbor, Sharon, had become engaged. As soon as we unpacked the car she was at our doorstep, holding her ring up for my inspection. I looked at the ring and then at Don. He knew at that moment, his goose was cooked. Within a couple of months, whilst in London, he knelt down in the flat I had bought for my father, and he asked me to marry him. I said "yes" and smiled from ear to ear, as he slipped a beautiful diamond ring on my finger.

We married on August 7th, 1999, in Las Vegas! I upgraded from the Reverend Peter Love's Marriage Emporium to the Mandalay Bay's exquisite wedding chapel. My dear friend Ewa flew in and was one of two maids of honor, the other being Phyllis. Don's daughter Natalie was my bridesmaid. One of the proudest moments in my life was the instant that Jonathan gave me away. Don's son, Greg, was his best man. We partied all night and then returned to Newport Beach where we had a big reception.

After our marriage, we continued to go on extraordinary adventures. On one such trip, we set out to meet a dear friend, named Marta Vereker, and her husband. Years earlier, I had met Marta when she joined the Oscar Kolberg dance company. She had come in on a visa, which she subsequently overstayed. Before the authorities could deport her she found a man who married her so she could remain in the country legally.

I was working at Alfa-Laval in those days and on a few occassions I helped Marta out with money. However, after quickly divorcing her husband of convenience, Marta soon fell in love with and married a multi-millionaire, ending her need for any type of assistance. One of the homes she and her husband now owned, was a penthouse overlooking Sugar Loaf Mountain, and the beaches of Rio de Janeiro, Brazil.

We arrived two days before the world famous Carnival was starting. Marta, being a dancer, like myself, had an assistant ready to put a costume together for us. Dancers in the carnival could dress outrageously. In some cases, their entire costumes were painted on. Ours were a bit less risqué, but we felt sexy none-the-less as we joined the revelers. We danced for an entire mile, strutting our stuff for all we were worth. We didn't start until four in the morning and by the time the sun came up, we were completely worn out, or as we say in England, "knackered."

From Rio, we flew to Lima, Peru and then we went to see the famous ruins of Machu Pichu, followed by Lake Titicaca, where the native population still lives on the world famous, floating reed islands. We had to leave our shore side hotel, in the middle of the night, because of a local labor strike that was shutting the surrounding area down, and threatening to become violent. We bribed our way through checkpoint after checkpoint, until we made it into Bolivia. There, we visited the ruins of the Tiwanaku civilization that predated the Incas by thousands of years. The world's first known brain surgeries were performed by this surprisingly obscure civilization.

From the time of birth, Tiwanaku babies had their heads compressed with planks and bound in a manner that was determined by which class of society they belonged to. As they grew, it is logical to assume that they suffered from intense headaches, which they attempted to relieve by drilling holes in their skulls. I greatly doubt that the drilling actually helped, but there is no shortage of skulls that demonstrate their prodigious use of chisels.

These adventures were wonderful experiences for Don and I. Our bonds grew stronger and our love deeper as we traveled the world for weeks at a time. Every now and then I would take a moment and reflect on how my life had changed. I had reached the pinnacle of wealth and success, before, only to be thrown into the pit of despair. This time, there was no fall from grace.

We settled into married life, as Jonathan started his senior year. After such a rough start he had ended up loving his high school. Amongst other things, Jonathan was quite involved in theater and was a budding lighting technician. One day a middle school was putting a play on in the high school auditorium and Jonathan was helping out. A friend happened to have brought a knife with him, which at one point he handed to Jonathan, to look at.

Precisely at that moment, some of the kids began making noise and the director yelled at Jonathan to silence them. Jonathan told them to be quiet and wagged the knife at them in the process. He did it as a joke but this being the time of the horrific Columbine incident, no one laughed.

A school official saw him do it and things escalated to the point that the police were called. Before we knew it, the vice-principal of the high school was expelling Jonathan from the school.

I was furious. I knew Jonathan was telling me the truth. Jonathan was no angel and he had done things his first year or two that had placed him in the vice-principal's office before. However, he had matured and was intent on having a great senior year. Instead, he found himself expelled. Jonathan and I both told the vice-principal that he was wrong, but he just assumed Jonathan was a rotten kid, who had no place in school.

I looked the vice-principal in the eye and told him he was making a horrible mistake. Jonathan was a great kid and he would graduate with his class whether the vice-principal believed in him or not. We walked out of the office and I gave my son a hug. I took him by the shoulders and told him that I believed in him. He was going to have to deal with the circumstances, but one way or the other; we'd prove he was innocent. In the meantime he'd have to go to an off-campus classroom for problem kids. I would not let him quit.

Later, Jonathan would tell me that it was my faith in him that gave him the will to keep going. Whether it was my faith or his true character shining through, instead of dropping out, like the vice-principal had predicted, Jonathan buckled down and hit the books. In the meantime, finally we were able to speak to the kids involved in the incident. The police dropped the case once they realized that Jonathan had been telling the truth.

In the spring of his senior year, Jonathan was officially reinstated in school and graduated on time with his class. He received his diploma from the same vice-principal who had written him off. Jonathan took the diploma, and leaned in to make sure the smirking vice-principal heard him clearly, "I told you I'd graduate... asshole". Thankfully, I didn't know until much later, what he had said.

While Jonathan and I were going through our travails, Don was as supportive as he could be. Like me, he believed Jonathan was telling the truth. Though it was a traumatic experience, we all came out of it stronger. Jonathan knew that he would never have to question our commitment and love for him. Likewise, he had proven himself to be exactly the high character young man we believed him to be. Through it all, Don was there to support me and our love continued to grow.

78

Globetrotting
(2000)

Once Jonathan and Greg graduated from high school, Don and I traveled even more. Don and I made a point of going to places that were of intellectual interest to us. We visited the best art galleries in the world. There is hardly a significant museum that we did not visit. We walked through the most beautiful churches, cathedrals and mosques in the world.

Actually, I had to look at most of the mosques from the outside, as they did not allow women to enter. After a while I had to drag Don through the churches and cathedrals I so loved. Finally, he told me he was "churched out." Don was happy to go on cruises, where he could relax, but he asked that I do the overland trips with my girlfriends. Don was busy with a new project in the mountains South East of Los Angeles where we have a beautiful home set amongst tall pines and low oaks.

I am a city girl. If there isn't an art gallery within walking distance, I begin to get bored. I'm all for nature, but not when

I'm wearing a nice outfit, and I wear a lot of nice outfits. Excluding my time at Buzzard's Point, I have always wanted to live in a city. One of the things that keeps my relationship with Don alive and joyous is that Don has never tried to force me to adopt his life.

Don bought a shopping mall filled with shops that he set about remodeling. He loves doing drawings and then turning them into reality. We soon settled into a wonderful routine wherein we were together in Newport Beach and on cruises, but when Don went to the mountains, I went to London or off on one of my archeological adventures.

Without Don to escort me in London, I called upon the services of one of my best friends, Andrew Dutton-Parish. Andrew is not interested in ladies, but he is interested in opera, ballet and gala events of all sorts. Don is thrilled for Andrew to play this role in my life and it only enhances our relationship. I love the fact that Don is secure enough to allow me to fly around the world without trying to make me feel guilty. Likewise, I am happy to give him the space to do what he wants.

I have a wonderful consortium of lady friends who join me on my travels when Don decides to stay on his mountain. Don and I have been blessed with a young loving relationship at a time in our lives when we are mature enough to recognize that we each have different needs.

One of my more memorable trips involved my dear friend Andrea. A couple years after Don and I were married, Andrea and I set off on an adventure across Europe. Andrea had opened a store that dealt in artifacts from around the world. I have always loved the beautiful amber jewelry that comes from the Baltic shoreline. Don and I had been importing it since 1997, distributing it through a number of stores, including Andrea's.

Andrea and I decided to go over together in January 2001, and find some new sources. It is worth noting that few people consider January the ideal time to tour Europe. However, with snow chains at hand we would set off with no regard for rational thought. A few thousand miles later we returned and in effect flooded the US market with amber.

Don still goes on trips with me, but he is judicious about which ones. He loves sunshine, relaxing beaches and nice restaurants. I am more inclined towards ruins and cultural excursions. I can spend an entire day wandering through the rubble of a disintegrated fort just imagining what life had been like thousands of years earlier, in the very spot I stand.

One of my favorite places in the world to visit is Ephasus, Turkey. This is where Cleopatra and Mark Antony honeymooned. I feel a deep connection to this place. The first time I went there I had a feeling of déjà vu. I don't pretend to claim that I was Cleopatra in a former life, but I wouldn't be surprised if I was one of her cats.

79

ROLLING THE DICE
(2004)

I loved traveling but I was getting the itch to get back to work. Don was involved in his business ventures in the mountains but they did not capture my imagination. I wanted to do something in London. I could tell that the market was only going to go up and I felt there was a chance to make a killing if the right deals were put together.

Since I was spending the majority of my time in America, I knew I needed someone on the ground in London, to partner with. I called one friend and then another, but the types of projects they were aware of, did not feel right to me. I went to London to look around for myself.

I had offered the use of my flat to an old friend, and for a few days we were room mates. He told me about a real estate deal he was in town to check out. He took me to look at a number of houses he was thinking of buying and converting, as part of a five-year investment plan. I could see immediately that he was on to something. My gut told me this was the opportunity I was looking for.

Though Don did indeed provide a secure safety net, my independence remained paramount in importance to me and a key to this independence was maintaining my own hard won reservoir of savings. If this deal went bad, I could lose it all.

I had to think long and hard about whether or not I wanted to take such a large risk at this point in my life. Everything looked good, but what if the market fell out? I had gone through that before. In the early 90's my life had fallen apart, partly due to the collapse of the real estate market in Southern California.

I thought about it long and hard and made my decision. I joined the investment group and set about financing my flat, in order to raise the capital I needed. At the age of sixty-two, I was rolling the dice. We bought our first homes and got our crews to work. In less than a year, we finished the conversions and put the new flats on the market. We sold them all within a month. We had multiple offers and could have sold a hundred more if we had them.

While the first homes were being redone, we found a four-story home for sale in one of the most expensive parts of London. It had been bombed during the war and replaced by a house that was nowhere near as nice as those surrounding it. The owners had done a shoddy job of patching it up and it stood in sharp contrast to the beautiful homes surrounding it.

We bought the house and began the excruciating process of applying for permits. Our plan was to tear it down, dig out a large basement and then put five floors on top of the basement. The designs were beautiful, now all we had to do was build it.

While a crew of English workers started tearing down the walls, we found another opportunity, in the guise of two old renovated mews. Unlike the tear down we had just embarked upon, these side-by-side homes, didn't need to be torn down, just gutted and remodeled. The market was still going up and my gut told me that it was going to stay strong for a while. After a lifetime filled with ups and downs, I was ready to take one more chance.

We had a Polish crew working on our other properties. We knew that we had to move quickly. There were cracks starting to show in some sectors of the market. I knew from friends that worked in finance that something was up in the bond markets. More and more foreclosures in America were starting to mar the performance of the bundled mortgages that had been sold and resold around the world. The London housing market was still going up, but I was nervous as to how long this could last.

The mews project was progressing perfectly but we were having problems with our expensive tear down. After we dug out the basement, one of the neighbors complained that we were weakening his foundation. We had to spend a month fortifying the basement walls. Time kept passing and we still had a hole in the ground.

80

PERFECT TIMING
(2006-08)

We finished the remodel on the mews and found a number of eager buyers waiting. However, when I went to visit the site of our teardown, I found the crew more interested in drinking tea than pounding nails. In order to insure things would move faster, we brought the Polish crew over to augment their efforts. Pretty soon we just replaced the original crew and from that point on the house began to rise before our eyes.

Finally, we sank the last nail into the roof and we found ourselves in possession of a most extraordinary home. It was absolutely gorgeous. We listed it immediately, in the spring of 2008. I could see that other premier properties were starting to stall and prices beginning to drop. In America, talk about foreclosures was starting to become a daily topic on the financial news.

We kept our price high and just when we thought we might have outsmarted ourselves, we caught a bite. We negotiated back and forth and finally in August 2008, the mews project and our multi-story home, both closed escrow. Barely a month later, the Lehman Brothers collapse sent the world's financial and real estate markets into a free fall. We had rolled the dice and won. I had turned my father's old flat into ten homes and a small fortune. We sold our properties for millions more than we'd projected, and we had exited the market at exactly the right time.

At the age that many people are afraid to take any chances, I had just risked all of my personal money, and come out a winner. I was married to the man of my dreams. My son was on track to become a surgeon and his lovely wife Aubrey was on her own path to becoming an orthodontist. I was so proud of all of them. Life was good and physically, I felt great.

A short time after this, I got word from my doctor that my latest mammogram had shown that there was a problem. I went in for additional tests and I was told that I had cancer. My doctor told me I needed surgery as soon as possible.

81

REFLECTION
(2008 - 2010)

After a lifetime of struggle, battling cancer was just the next challenge on the horizon. I attacked the cancer with everything I had. I researched every form of treatment and ultimately worked out a modified program that felt right to me.

This time I faced my illness with the love and support of a wonderful husband and a mature loving son. I didn't allow the fog of depression to settle into my mind. Finally, I was in control of my life on every level that I could be.

I had the surgery, but due to the fact my cancer had been caught when it was microscopic in size and still in Stage 1, I made the personal decision to refuse radiation. I have a daily pill I will be taking for the coming years, but aside from regular hot flashes and aches in my joints, I feel no lingering effects. I continue to credit my workout and nutritional programs, with helping me carry on at the level I am.

Even if the treatment failed, it would not ultimately matter. The betrayals that marked my relationships in the past, from my father, to Wheeler, to Severin, were no longer a concern. I had lived to love the man of my dreams. I had traveled the world. I had raised a wonderful son. I had dared to roll the dice as an entrepreneur and I had won.

As I write these words, in January of 2010, my health feels fine. No one knows how long any of us will be here. After I heard my diagnosis, I had an urge to share my story with other women. This book is not for me. It is not easy to relive some of the sadness I've gone through, but I do know what it takes to overcome hardship.

I also know that it is never too late to find true happiness nor to live life boldly. I have paid the price to be here and I continue to do so. When I wake up tomorrow, I will put on my workout clothes and exercise until I am dripping with sweat. I will hug my husband and whisper into his ear that I will love him for all time. I will call my son to tell him how proud I am of him and his lovely wife, Aubrey. When the day is done, I will work late into the night on my newest venture, until I can work no more, and only then, will I snuggle up next to my Don and go to sleep.

I meet many women who seem to think that life can have no more new beginnings once they reach a certain age. After I had given up any thoughts of finding the man of my dreams, I met the right Don, the only true love I have ever had.

We can remain relevant, and sharp, and alive, and inquisitive, and sexy, no matter how old we are. It takes work and there is a price to pay, but the other option is simply to drift away into oblivion and that is not something that I am ever going to do.

ADDENDUM

MY DAILY REGIMEN

I have decided to memorialize my daily regimen, in case it can be of assistance to some people. Please understand that this is my personal program. I am happy to share it with you but, as with any nutritional regimen, you should check with your own health practitioner, if you have any questions or concerns.

BASIA'S DAILY ROUTINE

- MORNING
  - Wake up
  - Put on pretty workout clothes
  - Drink a glass of tepid water with a wedge of lemon
  - Take a serving of pro and prebiotics
  - Drink a smoothie consisting of a mixture of the following.
    - Yoghurt
    - Aloe Vera (essential)
    - Blueberries
    - Pomegranate
    - Protein powder
    - Concord grape juice
    - Prune juice
    - Additional berries & fruit as desired
  - Do a half hour of work on the computer to allow for digestion.
  - Work out to a different tape on a regular basis.
    - I call this system MUSCLE CONFUSION
    - From yoga to aerobics to weights to Pilates
    - I find that the variety is beneficial
    - I exercise between thirty and sixty minutes per day.

- REST OF DAY
  - My key rule is NO JUNK FOOD
    - Though I do cheat with a few fries from McDonalds every now and then.
  - Cooked and/or raw vegetables are a must
  - Fish, chicken and turkey on a regular basis
  - Steak on an infrequent basis
  - I keep things as organic as possible
  - I munch on raw vegetables instead of crackers or candy
  - I drink a glass of juiced vegetables each day – here are my favorite ingredients
    - Beets
    - Apples
    - Celery
    - Carrots
    - Parsley
    - Chard
  - Exfoliate and moisturize with ALOE - all over the body
  - Water all day long but based on activity level so I don't drown my organs
  - Vitamins & Minerals
    - Multiple vitamin
    - Revesterol
    - Omega 3,6 & 9
    - Calcium
    - Vitamin D
  - I try to spend ten minutes a day in the sun, soaking it into my skin.
    - When I fail to do so, I pull out my trusty tube of fake tan.
    - Always use sun block

In general, it is important to be realistic and allow yourself to fall off the wagon every now and then. Variety is beneficial. I also eat eggs, avocado, cheese and organic bread. I have never been big on sweets though, in moderation, almost everything is fine.

THE POLISH HISTORY LEADING TO WWII & THEIR ROLE WITHIN IT

Strong Kings and warriors originally carved out a powerful Polish nation but by the time the bloodline reached my parents, weak royalty and merciless crusaders had combined to erase Poland from the map. After a subservient century, Poland reemerged for twenty exhilarating years between World War I and II. However, a few years before my birth, Hitler was threatening to invade Poland and again, take lands the Germans had always coveted. Once he had done so, his Nazi stormtroopers would take the rest of Europe and rid it of all but the master race, eliminating the Jews, Gypsies and then the Slavs. This is the story of the origin of this age old battle between the Germans and the Poles.

In the 10th Century, the wooded slopes and flowered pastures of the Baltic region, of central Europe, were comprised of a number of Slavic tribes ruled by a pagan Piast from Polonia, named King Mieszko. He was the first crowned King of Poland, establishing his rule in 966AD. The King had taken the leadership from his father, and greatly expanded the new Kingdom of Poland's lands.

Their valleys and plains had been protected by geography for many years, but the great power of the Roman Papacy was close at hand, threatening King Mieszko's new borders. The neighboring Bohemians had already bowed to the inevitable and accepted the Christian God of the Germanic people to their west.

King Mieszko was not afraid to fight. He had led many successful battles. However, he was pragmatic in nature and his desire was to craft a strong and peaceful future for his young kingdom. He also could not deny that there seemed to be true benefits for those aligned with the Christian kingdoms.

Their alchemists had better techniques for melting metallic ores and crafting tools and weapons. Trade caravans poured into their interlocked markets; bringing ivory from Africa and spices from the magical mountains of India. His own markets had seemed rich until he had heard first hand accounts of the bursting bazaars of cities such as Rome and Berlin.

King Mieszko could see the impending danger. His army was strong but tired of warfare. At their core, the Poles were farmers and artisans. The Germanic tribes pushing against his borders were more militaristic. Also, they had an unending source of volunteers, mercenaries and, most importantly, armored knights who worked at the bequest of the Holy Emperor. These knights came from a mystic order, first started during the Crusades, in Jerusalem. They were ruthless and apologized for nothing. Anyone who opposed them, opposed God, and thus deserved a swift and painful death.

These mighty knights were first commissioned to protect hospitals for European crusaders and travelers to the Holy Land. Over time, their taste turned to spreading Christianity throughout Europe; whether or not the pagans wanted it. Though they numbered only 1,000 members, they were more powerful than armies many times their size. The Teutonic knights were the 'special ops' troops of their day.

King Mieszko made a sage political move and allied his interests with those of the all-powerful church. He married a Christian Princess, named Drobawa, daughter of the Bohemian King next door. Drobawa replaced the eight pagan wives in King Miezko's harem and then proceeded to replace the pagan idols in the castle, with Christian crosses.

King Mieszko was baptized and gave his allegiance to the Holy Catholic Church and the Christian God. At the same time he signed a mutual defense pact with his new father-in-law. This alliance, combined with the gratitude of the Pope, kept Poland safe, for the time being.

Over the next hundred years, the King's power became dispersed between four independent and relatively equal Dukes. In 1190, the province of Mavovia was attacked by pagan Prussian forces, from the east. Due to a feud, the Mavovian Duke turned to the Teutonic knights, instead of his Polish brothers. The Duke of Mavovia promised the knights the town of Chelmno, and the lands surrounding it, if they could defeat the Prussians.

The Teutonic knights came in with the Pope's blessing and their maces swinging. They tore through the Prussian forces and took over the lucrative amber trade, which the Prussians controlled. The Teutonic knights went on to turn Chelmno into, in effect, a Germanic kingdom. Large numbers of their countrymen poured into this new land and the native population was soon outnumbered.

Over time, the rulers of the other Polish provinces united under the leadership of Kazimierz the Great, who wanted to take back the lands the Mavovian Duke had given away. A mighty war ensued. By the year 1410, the fate of Poland hung on the outcome of a battle to be fought at the base of a prominent town, known as Grunwald.

The thousand strong army of Teutonic knights marched out in their traditional white tunics, black crosses emblazoned on their chests. Waiting to meet them was a combined force, made up of Polish and Lithuanian soldiers. The Knights had not anticipated such a powerful alliance and in the ensuing days their forces were decimated.

The knights retreated to Chelmno and fortified their key towns. In 1460, they were struck again and driven out for good. The Germanic immigrants, now living there, were absorbed back into the kingdom of Poland. There they would stay for hundreds of years, a prize constantly sought after by the rulers of their original homeland. Early in the 20th Century, the nation of Germany rose up against all who would defy it, and for a short time took the lands it saw as its own.

When World War I ended, Poland again breathed its own free air. However, while the Poles were rebuilding their roads and cities, a new tyrant was building the greatest army the world had ever seen.

Adolf Hitler shouted out the legends of the Teutonic knights. He once again dredged up Germany's ancestral claims, to vast tracts of Polish land. Just as the knights had done, he would lead the Germans on a mission to clear the land of all but the 'master race'. First, he would rid Poland, followed by the rest of Europe, of the Jews, the Gypsies, and then the Slavs.

Many people are unaware of the integral role the Polish Army played in World War II. Two Polish divisions were dispersed out of the mid-east while a squadron of Polish pilots, who had escaped to England, were responsible for some of the most daring and dangerous missions of the entire war.

Knowing in most cases that they would never see their families again, the Poles knew no bounds as to the risks they would take in order to fulfill their mission. Polish soldiers and even civilians were routinely parachuted back, into their homeland for disruptive guerrilla attacks, in terrain they knew far better than the Nazi invaders. Their ongoing efforts, made Hitler greatly regret allowing close to half a million Polish soldiers, officers, intelligentsia and peasants to escape and take arms against his army.

While the Polish army was quickly driven out of the country, 16,000 German soldiers were killed in the invasion. Through the course of the war Germany, would lose an average of 500 soldiers per month trying to keep the Polish people in check.

The only country that came close to Germany in drawing the ire of the Polish people was Russia. Eventually, the Polish people would be sold out to the Russians at the Yalta conference, a wrong that would not be righted for nearly 35 years. However, during the war the Poles felt they were fighting for their freedom and no one fought harder.

Karolina's own family paid a horrific price. Karolina had been one of 14 children and one of those was her twin brother. One night, in the Russian prison camp, Karolina sat up like a bolt, out of a dead sleep. In that moment she knew that her twin brother had died.

Later, she would discover that he had been killed at that very time, on a mission for which he was post-humously awarded, with the Polish Army's version of the Medal of Honor. Of the 14 children in Karolina's family, eleven would die in the war. Only Karolina and two of her sisters would live through it.

Printed in Great Britain
by Amazon